Can Y *Fluent* In Success?

CW00530045

A fresh perspective on business coaching through the lens of an international rugby leader

DAMIAN MCGRATH

All rights reserved; no part of this publication may be reproduced or transmitted by any means, electronic, mechanical, photocopying or otherwise, without the prior permission of the publisher.

First Edition 2023. First published in Great Britain in 2023.

The author has made every reasonable effort to contact all copyright holders. Any errors that may have occurred are inadvertant and anyone who for any reason has not been contacted is invited to write to the publishers so that a full acknowledgement may be made in subsequent editions of this work.

Design Copyright 2023 Tidbury Media. (www.tidburymedia.com)
Text Copyright 2023 Damian McGrath

"Damian is an exceptional rugby coach with Skills Development his forte. He was the linchpin of our team's success, a mentor who transforms raw potential into polished performance. With an innate understanding of the intricacies of the game, he possesses the ability to dissect every aspect. His dedication to honing the skills of his players was unwavering, instilling a unique passion for detail. He combined his technical expertise with an uncanny ability to inspire, creating an environment where the young players flourished. Under his guidance, players evolved into confident and agile athletes. I am eternally grateful for his contribution but the players more so, an excellent skills coach isn't just a teacher; they're a game-changer, shaping the future of the team one skill at a time. Thank you."

RUPERT MOON
General Manager North Wales Development Region
(Former Llanelli and Wales RU)

CONTENTS

FOREWORD

With an upbringing in Rugby League, a stint developing the best young players in England and Wales and then leading a variety of different nations including Samoa, Canada, Germany, and Kenya few coaches can be seen to have had such a wide impact on developing players and rugby systems around the world.

However, what makes Damian truly stand out as a coach is his remarkable track record of success. At the highest level he has won with a mixture of nations that can be seen to have more in differences than in similarities. Vastly contrasting budgets are matched by the gaps between societies and cultures as well. Therefore, when it comes to lived experiences in elite level sport, Damian is right up there.

Looking back, I first met Damian over 20 years ago when I was a young university student looking to forge a career in the unforgiving world of International Rugby Sevens for England. Damian was a coach whose attention to technical core skill detail was beyond anything I, or any other player at that time, had experienced before. After retiring from playing, I coached with him as he assisted and mentored me in my role as England Sevens Head Coach. Then to complete the circle I finally spent a number of years coaching against him on the World Sevens Series.

I have therefore seen Damian from all sides and reflecting now on how he has achieved success in such an eclectic mix of environments there are two key characteristics that stand out. Firstly, he knows the game and has a crystal clear identity as a coach, based on the central importance of core technical skills. He is relentless in this message and backs this up with an endless number of practices to stimulate players learning. Secondly, he is as authentic as can be, a genuine and humble Yorkshireman which when combined with a natural talent for story telling enables him to connect with players at the 'person' level.

He connects with the person and coaches the player and with over two decades of success all over the world I cannot think of anyone more appropriate to write a book on the fluency of success.

SIMON AMOR

———

Simon Amor is an accomplished English rugby coach and former player. He captained the England National Rugby Sevens team and played for clubs like London Scottish, Gloucester, London Irish, and London Wasps as well as being a Cambridge Blue. Amor has excelled in sevens rugby, winning silver at the Commonwealth Games and being named IRB Sevens Player of the Year in 2004. As a coach, he led England Women's Sevens and later became the longest-serving head coach of the England National Rugby Sevens team. He also coached Great Britain to an Olympic silver medal in 2016. Amor briefly served as attack coach for the England Rugby team before taking on coaching roles with Hong Kong and currently heads the Japan National Rugby Sevens team, marking his third national sevens coaching position.

THANK YOU

Two of the most common words in the English language are 'Thank You'. They are often used but rarely said with the sincerity that they should be. How can we operate without using them properly?

Our reliance upon, and thankfulness for, the help of others can be beautifully described using the saying "No man is an island". It is the famous quote from John Donne, a 17th-century English poet and cleric. It is taken from his work *Meditation XVII.*

As much we all like to think we can do it all ourselves and make our own way, it's just not true. In our journey through life we often encounter challenges and obstacles that we cannot overcome alone. It is during these times that we come to realise the significance of leaning on others for support.

My Mum and Dad gave me what we all need – unconditional love and support. My wife Deborah is my rock, she has shared the ups and downs without complaint and never stopped believing. My children, Niamh, Tom and Joe have suffered having a dad in professional sport but are the most important thing in my life.

Where would I have been without Paul Daley and Graham Murray who not only gave me a chance and their time, but coaching and life lessons money can't buy, I owe them a debt of gratitude words can never express. Brian Ashton, Tony Rea, Ged Glynn and Terry Sands have always given me their time and support but most of all their friendship. In Canada my great friend, Karl Fix, has never stopped giving his time for rugby and his support for me has not stopped since the day I was lucky enough to meet him.

Leon Lloyd and Barrie McDermott were two outstanding players, I had the good fortune to meet and coach. Both of them suffered injuries and setbacks that would have floored lesser men, both refused to allow the setbacks to define them and both went on to become outstanding and successful men in life after sport – Barrie in the media and Leon in the boardroom. But what I most admire and love about them, is that despite their own problems they are always looking to help others. I am so grateful for their enduring friendship.

Joe Lydon was one of rugby league's most famous players. He went on to be just as successful in both codes of rugby as a top-level sports administrator. Mentor, confidant, critic, comedian and most of all the greatest of friends.

Last but not least are the players and staff who have made my life in sport so worthwhile. I am in awe of the people I have worked with. So much talent, so much enthusiasm and too many to name but I hope they know how grateful I am.

When we are in need, whether it's emotional support, advice, or practical assistance we feel gratitude for the kindness and generosity of those who come to our aid. Recalling memories in writing this book has simply brought home to me what a lucky man I am. At important steps on my journey I have had the good fortune to meet some wonderful people without whom I could not have persevered or moved ever onwards. I am eternally grateful for their friendship, their expertise and their time.

DAMIAN

INTRODUCTION

*I would like to begin with a disclaimer, **this is not** a "How to" book. It isn't trying to be a guide to coaching and leadership.*

It is simply my reflections on 40 years of coaching, teaching and leadership. It is not meant to be a life-story but rather how I approached my journey that took me around the world, the lessons I learned and the common guiding principles that have stood me in good stead. Unlike the multitude of social media gurus, I would never claim to be an expert or a world leader, in fact the longer my career has lasted the more I realise how much I don't know and the more curious I have become.

Of course, if you want advice there are literally millions of "self-help" books. Many written by some very educated and learned men, with titles that really do try to tell you 'How to be a Great Leader', 'How to be a Great Coach' or 'How to be a Success in Life, Business or Sport'. Look in any bookstore, look online and you are spoilt for choice. There are podcasts, You-Tube videos, webinars and blogs, all of them vying to point out the way forward. The most enticing are the autobiographies of outstanding Coaches and Leaders, people that really have been successful. I, like so many, love reading about the life and careers of the great sporting and business icons, but for me it has never been particularly what they did, but how they did it.

Given that there is such a surfeit of good information available it must be straightforward becoming a successful coach or leader? Buy the books, listen to the podcasts, attend the courses, get on webinar's, check on what the greats did and off you go. But that is not enough. Yes, the guiding principles are all there but unless you adapt them to the circumstances you find yourself in, they are meaningless. You can't simply copy someone else's approach; you must discover one that fits you and your situation.

One thing I do believe passionately is that coaching or leading, if done properly, is an art. It is often supported by science, but it is essentially driven by feel and personality. It is why it is so difficult to quantify. The fluidity and volatility of life means you need to adapt and change on the fly, often making decisions based on feel as well as fact. That is where experience plays a huge part. The opportunities I had as a beginner to observe and question some of the best coaches around were invaluable. I would turn up wherever I felt it was worthwhile, if they were opening an envelope, I would be there to watch how they did it! Watching, listening to, and if possible, questioning experienced practitioners gives a perspective and a view the written word cannot match. My subsequent experiences of working with and for some of the best in their field gave me priceless work and life lessons that I have never forgotten. The skill of course is in not blindly following what they do but in adapting your approach to your own circumstances.

My story certainly isn't headline grabbing enough or unique enough to fill a book but to give context to my reflections I must mention my roller coaster journey, which is best described by Harry Chapin who so eloquently said in his song 'Circles' – *"No straight lines make up my life and all my roads have bends, There's no clear-cut beginnings but so far no dead ends"*

So where to start, what prompted me to even contemplate putting pen to paper or think I had a view worth considering. Two conversations were the key.

I returned to the UK for a quick holiday and was having a beer with friends. We were talking and shooting the breeze about life in general, when one of them asked me about my language skills, given that I'd lived and worked in so many different countries over the last few years. I had to truthfully, and shamefully, admit that I was no better now than when I started. He laughed and jokingly said *"Well at least you can say you're fluent in success"*.

It was a throwaway line, said in jest but it got me thinking. Can you be such a thing? Can you work in different cultures, different languages and adapt your way of working to be successful? But that prompted me to think about how I would define success? The answer to that question was made clear to me the following month.

I was invited to speak about team building to group of local council employees in Victoria, the capital of British Columbia in Canada. They were not sports-people, they had no connection to rugby, so my status as a High-Performance Sports leader, the Head of Rugby Canada's Men's Olympic programme, held no great meaning to them, especially in a country where Ice Hockey is king. Consequently, I was hoping that the organiser would give me a big introduction, listing my achievements, inflating my importance, making me sound like I was someone worth listening to, but she simply said;

"This is Damian McGrath; he has worked all around the world and has a reputation for leaving places better than he found them".

I have to say, my initial reaction was, underwhelming. I am not sure what I was hoping for, but I think it was definitely a bigger introduction, something that would establish my credentials whilst of course listing any successes I may have had. But as I drove home afterwards and reflected on the day my thoughts turned more and more to the introduction. I obviously wanted something that pandered to my ego, but the longer I thought about it the more I came to the conclusion that in hindsight it was probably a better introduction than I could ever have hoped for. If that could even be half true, then I would view my coaching career as a success. In fact, I think it is the ultimate compliment, what more can any of us ask for, in any walk of life?

I have certainly had plenty of practice of operating in different circumstances. I went from teaching to coaching. Coaching children to coaching Academy age teenagers, and then teenagers to experienced internationals, I changed from Rugby League to Rugby Union at the start of the millennium when the two codes of rugby were still poles apart in approach and culture. Worked across all levels with England Rugby from Senior 15s, 7s and Under 19s. I was part of Spanish Rugby's International Coaching team for almost three years as they jumped over 20 World ranking places to establish themselves on the world stage. Two fantastic years in North Wales as Head of Rugby in a part of the country where English was not predominantly the first language. To be the first non-Samoan to be National Coach of Samoa in the South Pacific was unique, challenging and fascinating in equal measure. Head Coach in Canada was similar to being home but so different in many subtle ways. Head Coach in Germany, where language and daily life challenged me more than I expected and Head Coach in Kenya, which required a magician rather than a coach, I could fill a book on that experience alone.

In each one I have achieved a degree of success which prompted the books title. But what did I do to try and leave it better than I found it? What were the lessons I learned?

BACKGROUND

Sport has been in my life since day one. My mum and dad passed on their love of sport to me, my two brothers, Dermot and Anthony and two sisters, Anne and Cath. The girls enjoyed it but to us three boys it was all consuming. My youngest brother, Anthony, went on to play cricket for Yorkshire and England and as I write this, he is having great success as Head Coach of Essex. We are a sporting family.

I played everything available: Cricket, football, Rugby, tennis, table tennis, volleyball, Gaelic Football, anything that I could. Tiddly-winks, marbles, closest coin toss to the wall, my friends and I turned anything into a contest. I just enjoyed competing. I was pretty good at everything but probably the greatest living example of the phrase 'Jack of all trades – Master of None'. I dearly wanted to make a career in sport, to just spend all day, every day, doing what I loved, that was the dream. The finances of modern-day sport mean that opportunities are more plentiful now than in my teenage years, where only football offered that life. I made the decision to become a PE teacher because it seemed to me to be the closest thing, I could get to do sport all day, every day!

I still harboured ambitions to crack professional sport and I did sign as a Professional rugby league player (albeit not a very good one) but back then Rugby League was a part-time sport, everyone, even the big stars, had day jobs. I was and still am, fascinated by what good players did that made them different, I wanted to get better, and I saw players who had no more talent than I did, achieve more success. What were they doing, what made them stand out? What was the difference? This fascination and my teaching background was the start of what was to become a lifetime's journey in coaching.

It's impossible to know everything and it can strengthen your position in certain situations if you are honest enough to admit that you don't, but the expectation on any leader or coach is, as my mum likes to say, *"to know your onions!"* On all levels I would expect to deliver for my players and staff. To improve them as individuals and as a collective, I really need to know as much as I can about my subject. Everyday is an education, staying on top of rule changes, understanding playing and training trends, watching games and talking with other coaches. Reading journals and most importantly making time to listen to staff and players alike understanding them and their view of the game.

There are three types of coaches I have come across – followers, adopters and innovators.

FOLLOWERS are the safety-first coaches. They follow the norm. They are textbook coaches. Whatever is recommended by the industry they are in; they take that route. Following what they feel is the accepted path. They lack vision and their plan is usually a generic one.

ADOPTERS are the people who look at successful leaders or teams and adopt their way of operating. It is almost like being trendy. "Is this what winners do? – right I'm going to do it". It's the fashion of the moment. But just like any fashion it might not suit everyone. Adopting someone else's approach can cause as many problems as it solves. What if your team doesn't suit that approach? What if your team doesn't have the capabilities to operate in that manner? Those coaches have an idea of what they want to do but they use someone else's approach. As Quentin Crisp said, *"Fashion is what you adopt when you don't know who you are."*

INNOVATORS are people with a real vision. Their plan is based on the resources (people, equipment, money) they have at their disposal. Their approach makes the most of what they have. They explore different ways of doing things. They don't just accept that it can only be done certain ways.

I read a great story about Herbie Flowers. In 1972, Flowers was an in-demand session musician. He showed up with his double bass guitar and did what was asked of him. David Bowie had worked with Flowers on his famous hit *Space Oddity*, so when Bowie was producing Lou Reed's *Transformer* album in London, Bowie recommended Herbie Flowers. Reed gave Flowers a bar of music to play. In the moment, Herbie asked Lou if it was okay if he experimented a bit. He decided to do an overdub – using an electric bass to go 10 notes above the double bass track he'd already recorded. The result: the haunting backbone of *Take a Walk on the Wild Side*. A song you would recognise instantly if you heard it even if the title doesn't ring a bell. In 20 minutes, Herbie Flowers delivered a tiny bit of genius and ensured Lou Reed's career. Of course, it took more than 20 minutes. It was years in the making, building his craft and learning to see and to listen.

It's not always about being brand new, a good coach can adapt what already exists to create something different. I have tried hard to be an innovator, not doing something new just for the sake of it but always looking at different ways to approach challenges. I have had the pleasure to work for or with some very clever people, some who have been described as 'Maverick', simply because they were unorthodox, unconventional, or nonconformist.

'Different' seems to frighten people, they feel comfortable with the accepted way but the innovators I have come across and admired have a keen eye for an opportunity. They tend to have a creative mindset that enables them to come up with ideas and approaches that can challenge conventional wisdom They are not afraid to take risks and explore unconventional paths. They have a genuine curiosity and thirst for knowledge, which drives them to constantly seek new information, insights, and perspectives. They persevere and are resilient in the face of adversity. Like all successful people they learn from their failures, adapt their strategies, and keep pushing forward.

If you were cooking dinner and the only ingredients available were spaghetti pasta, minced meat, tomato sauce and Italian herbs, what would you cook? Given the ingredients the best you could do with them is surely Spaghetti Bolognese. You wouldn't try and make filet mignon or Chicken Kiev! But put this in rugby terms and so often you see coaches trying to play in a manner that doesn't fit their players or get the best out of their strengths. This may seem simplistic but finding the recipes that suit your ingredients is the first step when coaching a team.

The beginning is always meeting your audience where they are. This will help you to bespoke your offerings and allow you to structure your work in such a way as to allow them to move forward. In Germany for example I was convinced we could make better use of the talents we had by focusing on skill and workrate and abandoning the style of play they were attempting, which in my opinion didn't make the best of what they had.

1) I had to paint the picture – **Imagination** – most skillful team in Europe/ World, what we can achieve with that, how it will help us, it's the secret ingredient of all great teams and players. Imagine what we could be?

2) Then you tell them how we do it – **Illustration** – Strategy, tactics, skills, fitness. Examples and stories – show success

3) Stress how everybody can contribute – **Participation** – encourage thoughts and ideas, actively seek solutions and influence change

4) Then make the vision a reality, embed excellence as a way of doing things. – **Integration** – Police the approach, no cutting corners, peer pressure. Commitment, focus.

To be 'Fluent in Success' you have to innovate and that can simply mean making the best use of what you have wherever you are. The guiding principles of coaching never change but your approach will never be the same, because nowhere is the same. As Michael Palin said about his TV travel show; *"The more you travel, the more you realise your experience of life, is just one way of living."*

A MAN FOR ALL SEASONS

To really be successful with any group I think you have to be able to teach, coach, manage and lead. In my experience they are all inextricably linked.

So often you have to dip into one area or the other in your working life. Everyone has their own views on what each area means and it is important that you look at what they mean to you. As a Head Coach you are imparting knowledge or giving instruction, helping people to realise their potential, providing them with the means to improve and to develop to their capabilities. You are managing egos, organising training sessions, equipment and facilities, motivating a group of people to achieve a common goal. You will almost certainly be leading meetings, be a salesman, an influencer, a visionary, an advisor, a communicator, you will be expected to be decisive and trustworthy. The list, whilst not endless, is certainly long. So, to be all of the above what is needed? There is only one expression that has ever come to mind. A coach needs to be a "man for all seasons".

Robert Whittington described the English statesman and scholar Sir Thomas More (1478–1535) as a *"man for all seasons"*. More was later canonised by the Catholic Church and the expression was used by Robert Bolt as the title of his 1960 play about him. Integrity is the major theme of *A Man For All Seasons*. Sir Thomas More is tested to the extreme as he remains true to his conscience but in the end, he is beheaded by Henry VIII because of it. At school, we learned much about one of the most famous of Catholic martyrs.

St. Thomas More, was known for his unwavering commitment to his principles, even when it meant going against the wishes of those in power. He was a man of great integrity and intellect, and his ability to navigate complex political situations whilst remaining true to his beliefs made him a model of ethical leadership. *A Man For All Seasons* portrays someone who is not easily swayed by the changing tides of public opinion or personal gain, but rather holds fast to their principles and values, regardless of the circumstances.

As time has passed the term has taken on a broader meaning. It can describe a person who is successful and talented in many areas. Someone who's prepared to deal with a wide variety of situations, who doesn't get flustered easily, but keeps a calm, efficient demeanor even in a crisis. They prove to be reliable and trustworthy acting with assurance despite external pressures. They follow their conscience, and act correctly especially in demanding situations.

Ever since I read of St Thomas More at school, the broad description of a "man for all seasons" has always stayed with me – a man who is true to himself, who doesn't sacrifice his principles, no matter what the situation! In modern terms he is seen as a man who is ready to cope with any contingency and whose behaviour is always appropriate. I have seen many of these traits in the great coaches and leaders I have been lucky enough to meet or observe, so if I had to describe the perfect modern leader it would have to be as a *"man for all seasons."*

The big picture is straightforward. You have to know where you want to get to, have the know-how in your subject and then have the personality that can pull everything together in a way that allows success to happen

First off you need **VISION**. A clear sense of purpose. You have to know where you're going, what you want to achieve and how you want to do it. A great vision should inspire, bring everyone together and give direction. The most important, and often underestimated, element is you have to really **KNOW YOUR SUBJECT**. To lead a group, you have to demonstrate a knowledge and understanding of the business you're in. To improve individuals you need an eye for detail and an understanding of where everything fits as well as seeing the bigger picture. Most facets of modern life change almost nonstop. Sport is no different. To keep current and ahead of the curve, you need to be aware of your subject and how trends can, and do, affect it. Always be looking to learn, as soon as you become complacent you lose! Be curious enough to explore options, being prepared to adapt and innovate but never ignoring the importance of fundamentals. Finally, you need **PERSONALITY**, this is the ingredient that marks out the best from the ordinary. You need to **CONNECT** with people no matter their age, experience and outlook. You need to be a salesman; you need to be a great **INFLUENCER**; It wouldn't be far off the mark to say that you need to be a performer. The ability to understand, use, and manage your own emotions in positive ways – to relieve stress, **COMMUNICATE** effectively, **EMPATHISE** with others, show **PATIENCE**, overcome challenges and defuse conflict are a fraction of the requirements.

As I thought more about the modern take on the expression the more, I feel that the "man for all seasons" is a combination of different people.

1)   An Everyman
2)   A Journeyman
3)   A Craftsman
4)   A Salesman
5)   A Nobleman

An **EVERYMAN** is an ordinary character with whom players and staff can identify. They seek to do the right thing usually without a fuss. They have a "What you see is what you get" approach. Now it may seem I'm describing an average bloke, but to some degree that is what is needed. Someone who understands the point of view of their staff and players. Understands their situation, their position in the hierarchy, be it a star, a striver or a beginner. They are

RELATABLE, they understand the common struggles, challenges and aspirations of the people they coach This relatability fosters **TRUST**, empathy, and a strong connection between a coach, players and his staff. Everyman leaders are **AUTHENTIC** and genuine in their interactions. They don't put on airs or pretend to be someone they are not. This authenticity creates trust and **CREDIBILITY** among their team members. People are more likely to follow a leader who is true to themselves and shows vulnerability when appropriate. They are **APPROACHABLE**, creating an environment where individuals feel comfortable sharing their thoughts, concerns, and ideas. It promotes open communication, collaboration, and a sense of psychological safety within the team. They are **INCLUSIVE**. They understand that everyone's contributions matter, regardless of their background, role, or level of expertise. They make sure all team members feel valued and are encouraged to contribute their unique perspectives and ideas. But most of all an Everyman coach has the ability to empathise and **UNDERSTAND** the perspectives of their team members. They recognise that everyone has their own unique experiences, strengths, and limitations. This empathy enables the leader to provide support, guidance, and coaching tailored to the individual needs of their team members.

A **JOURNEYMAN** has come to be a chiefly depreciatory term in sport and is usually a thinly disguised insult. It's often used in boxing, where a boxer has adequate skill but isn't the calibre of a contender (think Rocky in the original movie). In football it describes a player who's played for numerous clubs during their career, they can do a job but they aren't valuable enough to keep long term. They are reliable but not outstanding. However, it is its true original meaning that resonates more with me. In medieval times a Journeyman was a worker who had learned a trade. The working Guilds recognised three ranks of workers beginning with Apprentices, then Journeymen leading on to be a Master. In parts of Europe, spending time as a wandering Journeyman, moving from one town to another to gain experience of different workshops, was an important part of the training to become a Master. In sporting terms, it is a coach who has served his apprenticeship and strives to be a Master through continuous education and learning. As a modern coach we must all see ourselves as a Journeyman striving to learn on a daily basis.

While the term **"CRAFTSMAN"** may not be conventionally associated with sports coaching, viewing coaching through the lens of craftsmanship highlights the dedication, expertise, and commitment that coaches bring to their craft, ultimately shaping and molding athletes into their best possible versions.

Just like a craftsman perfects their technique and skillset, a coach invests significant time and effort into mastering the principles, strategies, and tactics of their sport. They continuously refine their knowledge and understanding of the game, staying updated with the latest advancements and trends. A craftsman pays close attention to details to ensure the quality and precision of their work. Similarly, coaches meticulously analyze every aspect of their athletes' performance, including technique, physical fitness, mental preparation, and tactical execution. They focus on identifying areas of improvement and developing tailored training programmes to enhance individual and team performance. Craftsmen often create bespoke, custom-made products. Likewise, coaches adapt their coaching methods and approaches to meet the unique needs and characteristics of each athlete. They understand that individuals have varying strengths, weaknesses, learning styles, and personalities, and they tailor their guidance and support accordingly. Craftsmen often pass down their knowledge and skills to apprentices, ensuring the preservation of their craft. Similarly, coaches serve as mentors and guides, transferring their expertise and experience to their players and their assistants. They provide mentorship, guidance, and encouragement to help their staff and players develop not only their physical abilities but also their character, discipline, and resilience. Craftsmen are dedicated to continuous improvement and lifelong learning. They seek out new techniques, materials, and approaches to enhance their craft. Likewise, coaches strive for ongoing professional development, attending workshops, seminars, and conferences to stay up-to-date with the latest coaching methodologies and research. They constantly refine their coaching techniques to optimise player development.

It was Hemmingway that said *"We are all apprentices in a craft that no one ever becomes a master."* That surely sums up coaching. In sport the game evolves daily. We have to stay relevant and at the forefront of modern approaches. But that doesn't mean we change everything constantly. For all great craftsmen, foundational skills or the fundamentals are the bedrock upon which craftsmen build their expertise. They provide craftsmen with the necessary tools to execute their craft with proficiency, tackle challenges, foster innovation, maintain quality, and pass on their craft to future generations.

If I had to highlight something that has been a constant throughout my coaching journey it would be my devotion to the fundamentals, the basic skills of rugby.

Along with my great friend Ray Unsworth we coined a phrase in the early 1990's – "When all is equal skill is king". It simply meant that when players are as strong as each other, are as fast as each other and are as mentally resilient as each other, the difference was nearly always who was the most skillful. Ray was the Head Coach of the Wigan RL Academy and I was the Head Coach of the Leeds RL Academy. We were fierce rivals but good friends, indeed we were co-coaches for a time of the Great Britain Academy team. We met and swapped notes regularly. At that time there was little in the way reading material on coaching and skill practices. We wrote a skills drill book and travelled around League and Union clubs promoting it and talking about the importance of basic skills (fundamentals) and how they were usually the difference between winning and losing (the difference that made a difference'). In our experience the best coaches develop players who can do the simple things exceptionally well on a consistent basis. By coaching a solid foundation, players are provided with a platform to experiment, innovate and adapt their techniques.

Booker T. Washington said *"Excellence is the ability to do the common thing is an uncommon way"*. In rugby terms the common things are the fundamentals – catch, pass, grip etc. but it is uncommon to see anyone do them consistently well.

A **SALESMAN** has to be able to sell the dream, to get buy in from not only the players but also their support staff and the administration. No one will invest in something they don't feel they will get a return on. The first time a coach meets their new team they need to capture their attention and motivate them enough to get them on board for the ride. A good Salesman knows how to engage an audience and make their message compelling. Similarly, a coach who can "sell" their approach effectively can make the material more interesting and relevant, increasing player engagement and participation. I always sell the need to have World Class basics, (foundational skills) and for me to be successful I have to persuade them to let me teach them what they think they already know. To do that I have to **PAINT A PICTURE** of why the success we can undoubtedly achieve is dependent on it. Salespeople are skilled at highlighting the value and benefits of a product or service. Similarly, coaches can use **PERSUASIVE** techniques to communicate the value of their approach and the importance of specific topics or skills. If you can effectively convey the **RELEVANCE** and practicality of what you teach, you can motivate people to actively participate in their own learning.

If you can **ARTICULATE** your ideas persuasively and gain support from your colleagues it will make implementing new methods, or advocating for changes much easier.

By employing effective sales techniques such as **STORYTELLING** and positive reinforcement, coaches can **ENGAGE** people emotionally and foster a sense of commitment and dedication.

Everyone loves a good story and I must admit I love telling them. If they are relevant, authentic, informative and memorable they can inspire and motivate.

As a coach you often need to implement specific strategies, tactics, and game plans to maximise the team's performance. However, these strategies may not always be immediately apparent or accepted by staff or players. By utilising persuasive selling techniques, coaches can explain the rationale behind their decisions, address concerns, and gain buy-in from the team. While coaching primarily involves teaching and developing athletic skills, the ability to sell and persuade can greatly enhance a coach's effectiveness in recruiting players, motivating the team, securing resources, and creating a supportive and successful programme.

There are four key steps:

1)   The first step is to have a way of coaching worth following,
2)   Then you design and build it in a way that people will actually benefit from and care about.
3)   Next you tell the story to the right people in the right way. Your 'Change agents' demonstrating and selling its worth
4)   The last step is the key one that isn't always appreciated, the part where you show up, day-in day-out to lead and build confidence in the approach you have championed.

A **NOBLEMAN** is not a peer of the realm but in this instance someone who is admired and respected for their character. Generally, a noble person is regarded as someone who displays exemplary behavior, integrity, and a sense of responsibility towards others, they demonstrate qualities such as kindness, compassion, generosity, fairness, and humility. Noble individuals are often admired for their ability to inspire and lead others.

Now that's a lot to live up to! Of all the "men" that make up our "Man For All Seasons", this one is the most complex but probably the most critical. Your actions and words are how you are judged and received. To have a vision as to what can be achieved, to sell your way as the best way, to be a top-level practitioner is incredibly important but your actions and character are the traits which more than likely will decide if you can deliver success.

The specific qualities that make a leader "noble" can vary depending on the situation or the place. Top of my list would have to be the indispensable virtue used most often to describe Thomas More and that is **INTEGRITY**. Someone who is honest, does the right thing, and stays true to their values no matter the circumstances. But just as important is being:

Humble
Compassionate
Empathetic
Inspirational
Courageous
Resilient
Fair
Accountable
Curious
Wise
Decisive
Communicative
Trustworthy
Open-minded
Adaptable
Authentic
Respectful
Consistent
Patient
Generous

This list is nowhere near exhaustive but it shows being a noble person is incredibly challenging. It requires a strong commitment to principles and a huge degree of selflessness. A coach must prioritise the well-being of others and make sacrifices along the way. They face high expectations and constant scrutiny, as they are held to a higher standard. Upholding moral values and virtues in a world that often rewards self-centeredness is difficult. However, those who embrace "nobility" understand the immense positive impact they can have on others and the potential to inspire change.

So being a "Man For All Seasons" is no small task, the next time you think that being a coach is just picking the team – think again!

THE BEGINNING

My first real coaching job came with my first full time teaching appointment. It was at Shakespeare Middle School in Burmantofts, a district of inner-city Leeds.

The area was best known for its Boxing clubs and football but a new Headmaster had been recently appointed who was a stalwart of the Leeds and Hunslet Schools Rugby League association. Bill Crann wanted to introduce Rugby to the school and, despite my inexperience compared to the other applicants, my rugby league background got me the job. It was probably the most rewarding of all the coaching roles I have undertaken. The boys had no experience of rugby just the limited exposure on television (remember this was before Sky TV and its regular coverage). They were rough and ready and most were regarded as difficult to handle but they threw themselves into it with everything they had.

I had to start from scratch with, not just only the rules but, the basic skills of the game. It was a mixture of repetitive drills interspersed with lots of invasion games, which kept them entertained and allowed them to have lots of play but always had context. This was the first and certainly not the last time that the importance of basic skills was brought home to me. I have never made excuses for concentrating heavily on the fundamentals wherever I have coached and it began here as I explained the value of doing the little things properly and saw the benefits, as did the little boys starting off on their rugby adventure. We had relative success for a non-rugby school. All the age groups performed well but the U11's surprised us all by defeating some long-established RL schools to reach the final of the Leeds and Hunslet Schools Cup. This was no mean feat given the large number of schools involved and it gave participation in rugby at our school a huge boost. I remember the day well as the school hired two double decker buses, that were well over capacity, to take supporters and parents across Leeds for a final, which, although we lost, was a triumph for such a small middle school.

The lessons I picked up during my time at Shakespeare Middle School have stuck with me forever. The importance of valuing the efforts of everyone, the importance of fundamentals, the importance and challenge of making training not only educational but enjoyable. The importance of giving them a reason that they understood, always having a 'why'. Being able to set out why we needed to do something and painting a picture of the benefits.

I also got a lasting lesson on being careful of using analogies when explaining things. In the first ever game for our U10's team. I called the boys in and named the team and gave them their positions. The little boy whom I'd chosen as fullback had a perplexed look on his face. He came to me and said he was a little unsure of what to do and where to be. *"Don't worry"* I said. *"You know the goal keeper in football?"* He nodded and said *"yes"*. *"Well,"* I said *"he is the last line of defence and the full back in rugby is very similar."* A big smile broke out on his face. He said *"Ah I understand now."* So off we went to the recreation ground on the council estate where we played the games. It was a huge full size adult pitch that made all these little boys look even smaller. The game kicked off and as always seemed to happen, one boy got the ball and ran with it and was chased by the opposition and his own team, like a swarm of bees. This was the format for several minutes and possession changed hands a number of times but stayed in the same area. Then suddenly from this little chaotic gathering a bigger boy on the opposition burst straight through the line and charged towards our try line. I looked for the fullback he was nowhere to be seen. I looked but couldn't see him until I glanced at our posts. There he was, stood beneath the goalposts much as a goalkeeper would do in football. Well, I had told him that was his role, and he was following my instructions to the letter.

Now the young boy with the ball could have scored anywhere along the 70m try line but… It turned out that the opposition teacher had had a similar type of conversation with his boys, he had told them that if you break through the defence you run and score at the try line, but watch out for the fullback, he is their last line of defence, much like a goalkeeper in football, you have to beat him then score!! The young boy with ball was following his teacher's instructions. He looked up and saw our fullback dutifully guarding the posts, he could have scored anywhere but "Sir" had said I have to beat the fullback. So, ignoring the acres of space to score he made a beeline for the posts and was tackled by our fullback. The try scoring chance was gone. It was a great lesson in giving a clear message. Analogies are useful but can be counterproductive if not given context.

I loved every minute of my first taste of coaching, I really enjoyed seeing the children develop, not only as players but as young people. I got a great deal of satisfaction from the whole process but most of all I took a lot from the lessons it gave me. I had no great plan to take it any further but sometimes a chance comes along and it's your choice whether you take it.

DAMIAN MCGRATH

LESS IS MORE AND ENJOY THE MOMENT

As my playing career began to come to an end an opportunity
presented itself that I hadn't considered. I was offered the role of
Reserve Team 'player-coach' on a part time basis at my club,
Batley RLFC.

I had a natural interest in what was done and how it was done but I had had no great plan in mind to step into a coaching position. However, the idea certainly appealed. I was working full time as a Rugby League Development officer, coaching in schools on a daily basis but I was also fortunate to regularly meet and observe some of the sports leading coaches as part of my day-to-day work. I also got to spend time watching the National Squad preparing for games and tours and it had whetted my appetite.

I didn't have to think too long about Batley's offer and jumped at the chance. The club also did me, and themselves, a huge favour by appointing the former Leeds and Great Britain captain David Ward as Head Coach. David was a local lad who had had success as coach of one of the giants of the game, Leeds RLFC. He brought his knowledge, discipline and charisma to the team and it certainly had an impact. His organisation and value driven approach had a great effect on me as I watched closely how he handled different situations. It was the first time I had been exposed to an organised approach to weekly and monthly training. He planned and had a vision of where he wanted to be. This now seems to be so obvious but back then it was the exception, not the rule. There were no Strength & Conditioning coaches, no nutritionists, no positional coaches, no psychologists, just the coach. David without having any real training in any of the aforementioned introduced bits and pieces of things in his own way and it made a difference. Our personalities were completely different. He was and still is a forthright individual never shying away from the blunt truth whereas I preferred the arm round the shoulder smiling approach, but we complemented each other.

I can remember the first reserve game I was in charge of and can still see myself sat in the changing room before the kick off. 15 players all looking at me, waiting for my words of wisdom. Many of the players I had been a team-mate of just a few months earlier, I can remember feeling daunted, unsure of myself and making the big mistake of trying to say too much. I had the idea that a Churchillian speech was required but I just waffled. As we walked down the tunnel to the pitch one of the lads just turned to me and said *"less is more Damian, we just need reassurance"*. Probably the most appropriate words I ever needed to hear. We won the game and that season went on to win the Reserve team league and were narrowly beaten in the Reserve team Cup Final. It was a year when I could start to coach in the way I would have loved to have been coached myself. I was positive, I highlighted everyone's strengths and encouraged players to observe the way their mates played and read their movements. I tried to select players in positions based on what I thought they could bring to the team rather than just select them in the positions in which they had become pigeon holed. It was a wonderful time to make mistakes and learn from them. I found out very early that blowing your top and berating everyone when things go wrong is futile and negative. Talking to Senior players and asking for their insights and experience is gold dust and helps get their buy-in. Trying to be too innovative can be just as negative as being too conservative, small changes made the most impact and one of the biggest lessons was playing favourites doesn't help the team. I was selecting players who so recently had been team-mates and were still good friends. Sometimes, even when I knew I maybe should go for someone else I picked players based on personal relationships rather than on form. Despite falling into those traps, I learned my lessons and we finished the year with great success. Interestingly at the start of the season I still wanted to play and fully intended as player-coach to take advantage of the fact I was picking the team. Yet the longer the season went the less I selected myself. I played off the bench maybe five times in the whole season. I realised almost straight away that to coach properly and give the other players the feedback and information they needed required me to have an overview of the game that only observing from the sideline could give. The league success of the Reserves is no big deal in the grand scheme of things but it was the first trophy of any kind the club had won in 65 years yet when the whistle went in the game where we clinched the title, I raced down the tunnel to wait for the team to come back into the changing rooms. I had it in my mind that the on-field celebrations were just for the players. I didn't enjoy the moment with the players and supporters on the field. It was something I repeated in my next job as well, before I realised that if success comes after all the hard work we do over the course of a year then you have to enjoy the moment. Take the accolades, see the happiness and soak up the euphoria that winning brings. It's what makes it all worthwhile and the joy forms the memories you will carry with you forever.

KINTSUGI

On a slow train to Manchester in 1979 I was stuck with only a magazine to read. There were no mobile phones back then, no kindles or iPads or internet come to that. If you didn't have a book or a newspaper you were left with only your thoughts or staring out of the window.

Someone had discarded a magazine on household goods! I had no choice, look at it or daydream! As it turned out it made a lasting impression, an article stuck with me because I found its message so powerful.

The article was on pottery of all things. It was the Japanese tradition of Kintsugi. Where broken objects were not thrown away but fixed and made whole again. The story goes that the 15th-century Shogun Ashikaga Yoshimasa broke his favourite tea bowl; it was a one of a kind and couldn't be replaced. He sent it to China for repairs and was disappointed when it came back stapled together, the metal pins were unsightly. So, local Japanese craftsmen came up with a solution – they filled the cracks with a gold leaf and lacquer, making the bowl more unique and valuable. This repair elevated the fallen bowl back to its place as the Shogun's favourite. Kintsugi embraces the flawed or the imperfect. It teaches you that your broken pieces make you stronger and better than ever before. After all, our cracks are what give us character. I was so taken with the messages at the time I wrote them down. I suppose the fact I was in plaster from a broken leg gave it extra significance.

1) Kintsugi demonstrates that something broken can be transformed into something even more beautiful and valuable.
2) The process of repairing the pottery with precious metals not

only restores its functionality but also adds a new layer of beauty, celebrating the journey of resilience and growth.

3) The repaired pottery in Kintsugi becomes a testament to its history and the experiences it has endured. In life, the scars we carry can remind us of the lessons we have learned and the strength we have gained from overcoming challenges.

4) The process of repairing pottery requires care, attention and patience.

Whether it's reeling from an injury or rejection, disappointment can be transformed into something new. Kintsugi suggests many things particularly that we shouldn't throw away broken objects. When an object breaks, it doesn't mean that it is not useful anymore. We should try to repair things because sometimes in doing so we obtain more valuable objects. Each of us should look for a way to cope with traumatic events in a positive way, learn from negative experiences, take the best from them and convince ourselves that it is exactly these experiences which make each person unique. The breakage is an opportunity and applying this kind of thinking to instances of failure in our own lives can be helpful. Kintsugi makes something new from a broken pot. The imperfection, the golden cracks, are what make the new object unique.

As a coach Kintsugi reminded me then, and still does now, that failure isn't the end, you can repair it, you can build something new that is stronger, but the scars are there to remind of the challenges that you have overcome.

WHEN OPPORTUNITY KNOCKS

At the beginning of the 1990's, the Rugby Football League decided to introduce an Academy (U19) competition.

All the leading clubs began recruiting the best talent in their area and the games were highly anticipated. The blue-chip clubs, in particular, such as Wigan, Leeds, Warrington and St Helens spread their nets wider afield and recruited countrywide. Of course, this meant that the clubs would have to recruit coaches for these roles and the competition to be appointed was fierce. Buoyed by my success at Batley I knew I wanted more of the same and was ambitious to move forward and test myself at the next level. The introduction of the Academy competition suddenly offered opportunities to coach at a higher level, but getting an opportunity with so many other coaches in the running would not be easy. However, as I have found so often in my career, the impression you make on other people can have a far-reaching affect.

The Head Coach at Leeds was Doug Laughton, he mentioned in conversation to Paul Daley, under whom I'd played at Batley, that he was looking to appoint a young coach to his staff. Paul had kept tabs on my success as Reserve Team Coach at Batley and recommended me to Doug. I got a call to pop in and see him at Headingley. I realised this could be a major step up the ladder, I was full of hope and nerves all at the same time. I desperately wanted the Academy coaching job and knew it would be a wonderful opportunity. I met him in his tiny office next to the old dressing rooms at Headingley Stadium, as always, he had his customary cigarette in his hand. His first words were *"Do you want to be my Assistant?"* I was taken aback. Leeds had recruited some of the sport's greatest players. It was a 'who's who' of Rugby League. It transpired that his Assistant had stepped down for health reasons only the day before. Suddenly from hoping against hope to get a foot on the bottom of the ladder at Leeds I was being offered a job coaching at the highest level, dealing with World Class players on a daily basis. I think of that moment often. I wanted to go the top in coaching and here, right at the outset, I was offered the chance to jump right to the very top. Unbelievable, it was incredibly tempting but I knew in my heart of hearts I was nowhere near ready. We often see or hear of people being promoted beyond their capabilities; I knew it was too soon for me. I had too much to learn and too many mistakes to make before I could step up to that level. I said *"Thanks but I'd prefer the Academy job please"*. There was silence and then he laughed. He said that apart from his job it was the most important position in the club, *"Leeds' future and my future depends on its success."* Very profound words that have remained true wherever I have worked. Only a fool will fail to prepare the next generation. I have seen at first-hand, particularly in Canada and Kenya, how a lack of investment in tomorrow can have damaging long-term effects.

A COACHING HORIZON

I was on cloud nine. Just to be part of the Leeds set up was a dream come true.

We were only paid travelling expenses but it was worth so much more to me. As well as my Academy role I travelled home and away with the first team, sitting on the bench, watching how the players prepared and reacted in the changing room and on the field. There was more of a social life back then and the chance to talk rugby amongst many other things with the coach and the players gave me insights I would never have got elsewhere. The organisation of the team, the expectations, the words used, man-management, things that plainly didn't work and things that did. I spent every weekend writing up notes on what I'd seen and heard. The thing that sticks out to me now and certainly did then, was how recruiting star names isn't the answer to success. This all happened when Wigan RLFC were the undisputed kings of Rugby League. They were almost unbeatable and won the League and Cup and the World Club championship on a regular basis. In answer to their dominance Leeds had recruited coach, Doug Laughton, and then a host of star names in an effort to match Wigan. There were some genuinely amazing, thrilling games in this period played in front of sell-out crowds at Headingley but consistency was always, it seemed, out of reach. Doug's man-management style was old-school and he seemed to play favourites, this led to all sorts of disgruntlements in a squad full of large egos. In retrospect it seems obvious to say now but it was a perfect example of an unbalanced team. The 'Galactico' approach only went so far, there needed to be more, "piano pushers not just piano players." It stuck out to me then and is still relevant to me now, a team needs players who get through the hard yards and are the glue that hold things together; they build the platform for the star names to perform. On a personal note, they have always been the first people on my team sheet.

Leeds reached the Challenge Cup final at Wembley two consecutive years under Laughton, 1993 and 1994. Both against Wigan and both were comprehensive defeats. The '94 final featured an amazing try by Martin Offiah who went the length of the field leaving Leeds defenders in his wake. I remember vividly sitting on the bench at pitch side as he flew past taking our cup hopes with him.

The whole Wembley experience was a childhood dream come true. The anticipation in the city leading up to it, being measured for our Wembley suits, the travel down, the hotel, travelling up Wembley way, walking up the tunnel to see the old stadium packed to the rafters, all things I had only seen on TV and never imagined I would be part of, albeit in a minor role. I remember looking around as we walked the hallowed turf before the game and thinking I need more of this; I can't just settle for this as my career highpoint. I know many people have specific goals for which the aim, I didn't, I had a coaching horizon which I was moving towards, I didn't know exactly what it would bring but I decided that I would strive to be the best I could be and see where it took me.

But all that is an aside to my main role at Leeds, which was coaching the Academy. As in senior rugby, Wigan were the benchmarks in the Academy league. They were well drilled, well coached and full of stars of the future. In an effort to match them Leeds recruited strongly with players from across the north of England as well as local talent. This began a trend at the club that would build foundations for years to come.

In the first season I had my first real taste of pressure. We were simply expected to win, we had invested heavily in junior terms and an instant return on that investment was required. It was a steep learning curve, as well as that pressure to win, there was the little matter of the 'David and Goliath' effect. Quite simply every other club we played used the 'fancy Dan', 'big spenders' tag as a motivation to raise their game, so literally every game had a cup final feel to it. I needed to adjust and soon realised that picking the 13 best players wasn't the answer. Results were up and down. As the season progressed the better teenagers were promoted to the reserve team and Doug Laughton saw enough in four or five of them to give them regular places in the Senior team. So, more recruitment was required.

The Chief Scout was Bob Pickles a former player with Hunslet, who it seemed to me knew everybody and if he didn't know them, he knew someone who did. Bob had been responsible for all these bright young stars coming to the club. Our relationship to begin with was a bit frosty, I was sensitive to any criticism of selection particularly when results weren't great and I always felt Bob thought he knew better. I was wrong of course and it was when we had to bring in new faces to replace those promoted to the senior ranks that I learned the benefits of collaboration. I knew nothing of many of our new boys and had to rely on Bob for advice.

It was a watershed moment for me. I learnt that two heads are better than one, that everyone needs a sounding board and that any good team is combined effort. The team became just that and the season, and probably my career, picked up at that point. The influx of new talent was based on team needs. We finished in third place in the league but played some outstanding rugby to reach the Academy Cup final, which was played at Old Trafford as a curtain raiser to the Premiership final.

It was another fantastic occasion played at the home of Manchester United in front of a very big crowd. Despite losing, to Wigan of course, it ended a difficult first season on a positive note. However, it hammered home to me something I had already seen and was aware of but somehow still fell foul of. Because it was the end of the season and a showpiece occasion, all Academy eligible players were made available to me. So, all those young players who had been promoted to the senior team and reserves put their hands up to play. Four of the boys had just played at Wembley in the Challenge Cup final! I felt an enormous pressure to play the very best young players we had. This would mean leaving out some of the regulars who had turned our season around and got us to the final. To be fair to Doug he said he was easy with whatever I decided, but everyone I sought opinion from had different views. In the end I picked the star names. On paper it was a good-looking line up. It was an unmitigated failure. We played OK and didn't lose by much but it was nothing like the performances the usual team had been putting in. The big names were pretty anonymous and underlined the point that, once players move up, they psychologically leave that level behind. It still rankles me today that I made that mistake but it was a valuable lesson that would stand me in good stead further down the track.

I was aware of murmurings around the club that a better known, more established coach was needed to make more of all these bright young stars that Leeds were signing, so I spent the summer up-skilling myself in any rugby related area I could.

As a trained teacher I understood the benefits of planning and organisation, I was good with people and I treated players in the way I would have liked to have been treated when I played. However, I was still too nice, I wanted to be liked, I was terrible at giving bad news I avoided it where possible. With this in mind I undertook a two-year diploma in sports psychology. It wasn't so much the information we were given or the lectures we had, it was being given an opportunity in written form to articulate my thoughts and perceived shortcomings in the essays we were set. The topics brought out my thoughts on what I felt I was good at as well as my shortcomings. The feedback was invaluable we looked at coping mechanisms as well as areas to focus on.

Growing up I was almost terminally shy; I still prefer to sit in the background and listen rather than be front and centre even with people I know. But to move forward in life I knew I had to overcome this shyness to move forward. The answer for me was 'know your subject'. If you speak from experience and with knowledge to backup your opinions you are usually on solid ground. Stepping out of your comfort zone and being ill-prepared brings out insecurities in most of us. I am still fighting to overcome my insecurities and shyness; the trendy term is 'imposter syndrome' but I hark back to those lessons learnt regularly as they certainly helped on my way towards the horizon.

But the measure of a coach in any sport is their knowledge of the game and the application of that knowledge. I had responsibility for some of the brightest stars in rugby league. I had to improve them where possible in attitude, approach and skill. As I mentioned earlier the Academy Coach of Wigan, our biggest rivals, was my great friend, Ray Unsworth.

Ray and I both worked in rugby development in our respective areas. As such we met up often and talked for hours about rugby, about players, but most of all about skill. It seems strange now but at this particular time in the early 1990's rugby training was nothing like the modern scientific approach we see now. Both Wigan and Leeds had S&C coaches, which made them the exception not the norm. Both had full time players in a largely part-time sport. Keeping those full-time players occupied needed more than just fitness, running and playing touch and pass. Wigan's Head Coach was an Australian called John Monie, he had brought over the skills drills that were a regular feature in Australian Rugby League. Ray generously shared some of the practices and we used to sit having coffees and design our own. Again, it seems strange to relate it now but there were no resources at the time for coaches. The Internet was years away from being widely available and there was just the Rugby League Coaching Manual to help. Ray and I decided to publish our own book of skills drills. I also had the great good fortune to be appointed as liaison officer for the Kangaroos, the touring Australian RL team whose seismic impact I will also discuss separately.

So, the new season began, I felt I was wiser, better prepared and had the drills and practices that would make a difference. The recruitment was well thought out and as always Bob provided me with some great raw talent including a young gangly youth called Adrian Morley who lit up the early season before transitioning into the first team after only a few months. It was a spectacular season with the league title sewn up with back-to-back victories over St Helens.

It was a very satisfying feeling to win in such a competitive league. I had come to terms with the pressure of expectation I understood the need to articulate and agree the vision of the team and making sure everyone knew why we did what we did. We repeated the feat the following year. This time it was little different, Sky Sports, as part of its RL coverage, broadcast many of the games in a special Academy midweek show. It was wonderful exposure for the players but it also helped build my reputation as a young, up and coming, coach.

But as always there is more than one person involved. I mentioned earlier how things had improved after I worked out it is always a team effort. There was a higher investment in the team when everyone felt valued. Bob Pickles is, in my eyes, the best scout/talent spotter I have ever met but the rest of the staff in our little group at the time were themselves bound for greater things.

There were two guys in the Media department, Stuart Duffy, who joined Bradford Bulls as General Manager and was at the helm during their glory years in Super League. His young assistant was Danny Rueben who is now Head of Elite Communication for the England Cricket team. The physiotherapist in those first years was Dave Hancock who certainly did forge a stellar path. He joined Wolverhampton Wanderers, Blackburn Rovers, Leeds Utd, and then Chelsea all as Head of Physiotherapy before becoming the England Football team physio for four years. He then crossed the Atlantic to join New York Knicks amongst others before setting up a sports software company. Not to be outdone our Strength and Conditioner was a young Kiwi called Dean Riddle. A real 'can do' type of guy. Dean became National Team Fitness Coach for the England Cricket Team before becoming Head of Strength and Conditioning at Yorkshire County Cricket Club, Castleford Tigers RL, Sheffield Utd, and Leeds Utd. He then rejoined Sheffield Utd as Performance Manager. He was headhunted by Nike to join their training group in Oregon before joining the Seattle Seahawks (where he won a super bowl ring) in the NFL as a sports scientist in charge of special projects for High Performance Innovation. It would seem it wasn't just me who was looking towards the horizon with dreams of bigger things!

The following season was a strange one; the sport of rugby league was on its way to becoming Super League and there was in-fighting and political turmoil in both Australia and England as the different groups battled for control. For Leeds there were other problems. There was a bombshell regarding finances and the debt the club faced put its very existence in jeopardy. Results were disappointing and there was an acrimonious parting of the ways with Doug Laughton. He was replaced by two of New Zealand's most famous players, Dean Bell and Hugh McGahan. Dean would be Head Coach and Hugh, Football Manager. This was a real coup for the club. Dean had been part of the all-conquering Wigan team of the late 1980's and early 1990's before returning to play in the Australian NRL. Hugh was a star player for Eastern Suburbs in Sydney (now the Roosters) and captain of New Zealand. It was clear from the outset that they had a poor opinion of British rugby league in general. Standards on and off the field were questioned and we were all certainly put under the coaching microscope.

It was a daunting time as I felt they had come in with a closed mindset and already made up their mind that we weren't good enough. I saw it as a challenge and, fresh from a fact-finding trip to Australia, I was eager to prove my worth. As always Bob Pickles had brought a new group of talented young men to the club and we had another great year.

This was the first year of Super League and a combination of poor signings and players leaving, saw the Senior team struggling in the relegation places, indeed it got to a must-win last game of the season that saw Head Coach Bell come out of retirement and lace up his boots and lead the team to a victory that kept them in Super League!

In the Academy League, Leeds once more led the way. Whilst many of their predecessors were pressed into service in the senior team as poor results and injuries took their toll, the new group defied my expectations and we were worthy champions. In a new innovation for the inaugural summer Super League all Academy games were played where possible as curtain raisers to the main game. This was great for the fans who could see and support the stars of tomorrow, great for the players who got an opportunity to play in front of big crowds and great for a young coach trying to impress his bosses and make his way in the game.

Hugh McGahan would come into the dressing room and watch and listen. He was particularly interested in what I had to say, how I dealt with victory and defeat. In one particular game at our old rivals Wigan, we had a stunning victory in front of a very large and vociferous crowd, but only after surviving a late fight back. This was only made possible by slack play on our behalf and a mistake ridden last quarter when they thought they had the game won. I congratulated the team and praised their outstanding play but then reminded them of the perils of taking their foot off the gas and that whilst winning was important for the team, for each of them it was far more. It was to demonstrate they had both the talent and the mindset to play and succeed at the top level. *"That's what you have to prove to Dean and Hugh"*, I said, *"Have they watched that performance and considered you for the Senior Squad or has it told them you are not quite ready?"*

Unbeknownst to me Hugh was stood at the back listening, he congratulated me on a great win but was very impressed with what I had to say to the players. He asked if I would sit with Dean and himself in the coaches' box to watch the senior game, it was the first of many invitations and the beginning of my next step forward.

INTERNATIONAL RECOGNITION

What sporting child doesn't daydream of representing their country?
I was no different.

As a Student Rugby League player, I was incredibly proud to play for Great Britain Universities against France and for British Colleges against both France and New Zealand. But that was always going to be the pinnacle of my international achievements. I could never have dreamt about where coaching would take me or to what levels.

Coaching a very talented Leeds RL Academy team put me into a new spotlight. With it, of course, came the pressure to succeed. Over 65 players from the academy system during my time went on to play in Super League; if you are a RL follower then many of the names will be very familiar. Adrian Morley, Kevin Sinfield, Francis Cummins, Nick Fozzard head-up a long and impressive list. The teams' success reflected well on the whole staff and led to an opportunity for me to be part of the Great Britain Academy coaching staff with my good friend Ray Unsworth (the Wigan academy coach) and one of British Rugby League's best coaches of the recent past, John Kear. It was another opportunity to step up a level. I got a perspective on representative rugby, to see and feel the differences in approach compared to club rugby.

One particular trip that stood out was in Toulouse against France. We were the curtain raiser to a Senior International between France and Wales. The Welsh team was a 'who's who' of great players whichever code you prefer! Jonathan Davies, Quinnell, Devereux, Bateman, Ellis, Gibbs, the list went on, it was a privilege just to spend time in their company.

The advent of Super League brought a shake-up in the international coaching ranks. I had moved on from the Academy earning a promotion to the Senior coaching staff at Leeds. I thought my international coaching opportunities had probably come and gone.

I had one brief appointment as Assistant to another good friend, the late great, Mike Gregory, in an Academy International but I concentrated on coaching at Leeds.

In 1998 I received a call from the Head of High Performance at the Rugby Football League, Joe Lydon. He asked me if I would be interested in becoming Assistant Coach for the Great Britain Senior National team. The new Head Coach was my old friend John Kear and he and Joe had noted my work as assistant coach at Leeds Rhinos and felt I would be ideal for the job. I can remember almost floating home to tell family and friends the news. It was made doubly exciting by the fact the following year the Rugby League World Cup was to be held in the UK.

The home nations split into their constituent parts for the World Cup. England had a very strong squad. Andy Farrell (now head Coach of Ireland Rugby Union) was captain. We had a blow just before the competition when star winger, Jason Robinson, switched codes to join England RFU but still included such as Adrian Morley, Sean Long and Paul Sculthorpe among the group, plus a very young Kevin Sinfield as a surprise selection.

Part of the preparation for the competition saw us spend two weeks warm-weather training at Disney World in Florida (at Disney's Wide World of Sports resort). The Disney Corporation was very keen to get involved in Rugby League. They wanted to explore the promotional possibilities of a link-up with the Rugby Football League. I had no idea that such an exciting sponsorship opportunity would cause such bad feeling.

In February 2000, Head Coach John Kear, Manager David Howes, Head of High-Performance Joe Lydon and me headed to Florida as guests of Disney for four days. We were blown away by their welcome and treatment. The facilities were beyond our expectations; the access to behind the scenes at Disney World was fascinating. We dined and discussed our needs and requirements with Senior

Vice Presidents. We also were given VIP treatment in all the parks, which brought out the child in all of us. It seems crazy now but our trip didn't have universal approval back home. Many die-hards questioned the need for such a link-up. We were accused of having a "jolly" rather than fact-finding. I was surprised to field phone calls from journalists on our return digging for negatives, asking how we spent our free time whilst away and openly questioning the need to have a warm-weather training camp before a competition to be held in the cold of November. Of course, politics were behind it all. Factions within the game who wanted more say were using whatever they could as a stick to beat their rivals. Mickey Mouse was seen as a degrading partner for our sport!!

I had never until that time thought about or questioned my credentials to coach at international level, I was proud to be appointed and proud of how I had worked my way up the ladder, I felt it was because of what I had done not who I was. However, I found that some saw my appointment as a result of my friendship with John Kear and Joe Lydon and not through any achievements on my part. My lack of top-level playing ability was thrown at me several times as if that was some kind of stigma. I realised then that no matter how ridiculous it may seem, some people will always expect top coaches to be appointed based on their playing pedigree. Even now, over twenty years later, it is still happening. The list of great coaches in many sports who had modest playing careers is a lengthy one yet journalists and fans still trumpet the appointments of star players to coaching roles.

Despite the furore behind the scenes, the camp in Florida went ahead and was outstanding. The players had everything they needed to get the most out of preparation. The fields, the gymnasiums and medical facilities were better than anything we had in the UK at that time. We stayed in purpose-built housing used by the British Olympic Association and all our dietary requirements were met in full. It was as good a camp as could be planned or hoped for. Disney bent over backwards to make our stay memorable. We had VIP treatment at several theme parks and even the luxury of having the park opened one hour earlier just for us. For some of the evening meals we ate in a couple of special restaurants not normally accessible to the public. It was this last part that got the headlines back home despite it being on the players day off and not interfering with what we were there to achieve. We headed back to England knowing that there were plenty of people hoping we would fail.

Great Britain/England hadn't beaten Australia for several years. They were our opponents in the opening game of the tournament. It was a historic occasion as we were to play them at Twickenham, the home of the Rugby Football Union. The first time a Rugby League game had ever been played at the famous old stadium. The Aussies were strong favourites and despite a big effort from us they were just too good on the day. I think as I walked out with the team and stood with them for the National Anthem I was about as proud an Englishman as there was. I had never in my wildest dreams thought I would be such an integral part of a World Cup and represent my country as a coach. I remember thinking afterwards it couldn't get any better I had reached the pinnacle of my achievements – or so I thought.

A LEAP OF FAITH

Just after attending the 1995 World Cup final with the Australian team, Leeds RL offered me the opportunity to leave my development job and go full time onto the coaching staff.

It was promotion to Assistant First Team Coach, the job I'd turned down previously. My heart said yes, but was I ready? I would have to leave the security of my job with the local council and its benefits for a no guarantee, no promises, 'could be sacked tomorrow', coaching role.

I was highly ambitious but uncertain about taking the leap of faith, out of my comfort zone, into a world where it was sink or swim. I had been invited to Australia that summer as a guest of the Australian Rugby League. I used it as a fact-finding trip which Leeds RL had helped fund. My experience there left me in no doubt that taking the risk was the right thing to do. The chance came and I made the choice to take it. Leeds Rhinos entered the Super League era and Dean Bell the former Wigan and New Zealand star was appointed Head Coach, his first coaching post! Head Coach and Assistant Coach both new to senior coaching. We were both fresh and keen and full of new ideas. The team was a mixture of experience and many of my young Academy graduates. Whilst we didn't pull up any trees, we did reasonably well finishing fifth.

Enter Graham Murray. I was shocked when Dean told me he was stepping away from coaching the Senior team. He felt he would be best suited to taking over the Academy set-up at the Rhinos, which had continued to grow and prosper. It was a time of uncertainty for everyone, but the CEO, Gary Hetherington, was a believer in building a strong club with the right people and he simply wanted a new Head Coach to replace Dean. Graham Murray (Muzza), came from Australia with an already impressive coaching CV. His achievements in the high pressure, cut-throat world of Australian Rugby League pointed to a man who could take the club forward. What a coach! What a man! If ever there was one person who changed everything for me, here he was. It would be impossible to quantify his impact on me, the team or the club. His tenure laid the foundations for future successes for the club on the world and domestic stage. Most of all it was his off-field work that blew me away. He connected with everyone, the backroom staff, the players, the office staff, the supporters, everyone was given time and a smile. He made them feel a part of it.

Although I want to highlight his off-field approach, he really knew the game. He was a great tactician. He utilised my work on the basic skills to great effect. Always underlining their importance and where they made a difference. The environment he fashioned, encouraged and demanded success. For the first time I saw someone bring a team together and encourage player participation using humour, stories and valuing contributions no matter how small. He showed how to influence people and shape direction without ever losing full control. On reflection he was very autocratic, as I think all leaders must be. He asked for input and let the players have their say but he knew where he wanted to get to and how he wanted to get there.

We often went out for a beer after a game. When it became known that Muzza was returning to Australia to take over at the Sydney Roosters we would talk of the future and where I might want to go. He knew of my struggles with shyness and a preference to stay in the background. He also raised the issue of profile. In general, at that time all top coaches in most sports were famous ex-players. My lack of a top-level playing CV had been mentioned more than once when I looked around for roles, would it mean I was destined to be a number two forever, a supporting artist? He also didn't have an international playing background but he constantly referenced making people feel right about themselves and their game. He said, and I have found it to be so true, *"Everyone wants to be valued, everyone wants to have someone believe in them and everyone wants someone to make them feel as though they are improving.*" If you don't value your own contribution enough and don't believe in yourself, you will never improve players and they won't believe in you.

Graham led Leeds to the inaugural Rugby League Grand Final at Old Trafford, Manchester United's famous ground, losing in a close game to Wigan. The following year Leeds Rhinos won the RL Challenge Cup Final in style at the last final to be played at the historic old Wembley Stadium. He left for Australia to continue his success, with narrow Grand Final defeats for Sydney Roosters and then North Queensland Cowboys. Such was his reputation he was appointed State of Origin coach for New South Wales which in Rugby League coaching terms is about as high an honour as you could get.

In 2013 Graham died suddenly of a heart attack. The testimonials that followed his death were many and glowing. To read them told of a man that wherever he went, he made a difference and left places better than he found them.

As Leeds Rhinos' success grew the interest in their methods did also. Everyone wanted to know what was happening and all the staff were receiving recognition. As previously mentioned, in 1999 I was appointed as Assistant Coach for the England team. We had two victories in home and away internationals against France. The following year was the Rugby League World Cup on home soil. Although we disappointingly lost in the semi-final against New Zealand it was overall a wonderful experience. The chance to work with the cream of British Rugby League talent and prepare to play against Australia, New Zealand, Fiji, etc, was another great learning curve. The RFL had appointed a new technical adviser, David Waite. An Aussie who had a strong technical background. He opened my eyes even further on the small technical issues that can affect a player and a game. His mantra of *"it's the little things that matter because what matters are the little things"* has never left me.

It wasn't all plain sailing; he savaged my analysis and how I conducted my meetings. I was still less than comfortable speaking in front of a group. I didn't have the conviction I had on the training field and was always too general or off point. In fact, the step up to the highest level, working with the very best almost paralysed my approach. Every time I spoke, I had the feeling that I was a bit of an imposter that I couldn't really tell them anything of note. I was searching for something special, if it was too obvious it surely wasn't worth mentioning! Looking back 20 years I smile as the simple things are the staple of everything I do!

THE HEART OF THE MATTER

It's amazing where you come across great lessons on leadership.

Day to day life can throw up examples from the most unexpected of places. A man I came to admire and was so grateful for was a leading practitioner in his field, his detailed vision, empathy and honesty made a nightmare scenario, a challenge I could overcome. His manner and his messaging in a life and death situation was masterful. What more do you need?

In late August 2014 I returned home, happy and tired, from the World University Games in Brazil. I had been the Head Coach of the Great Britain Universities team that had just won Gold in the Men's Rugby Sevens in Sao Paulo.

It came at the end of gruelling Sevens season. I was Assistant Coach with the England Men's Rugby Sevens team that had just completed a tough eight months on the World Series criss-crossing the globe, followed by the Commonwealth Games in Glasgow which, with camps, had been another couple of months travelling, preparing and competing. I must admit that I was feeling physically in good shape. One thing we had done consistently as a staff was to keep up our own fitness levels by training hard on a daily basis. I felt good mentally and physically. I had always kept up my fitness levels. Despite being the oldest member of staff, I pushed hard on the rower and the bike to supplement the weights programme we followed.

Exercise has always given me a great sense of well-being and on return from Brazil I visited the gym after a couple of days to have an easy workout to aid my travel recovery. At the end of the session, I was sat on a bike pedalling slowly to warm down. Suddenly without warning I had what I thought was indigestion or heartburn, neither of which I had ever suffered from. It persisted for a minute or so. I wasn't worried as I didn't think it was particularly sinister and it wore off and didn't return.

The following day I had a Doctor's appointment for an unrelated matter. Once he had quickly sorted out my other minor complaint he asked about my health in general, I mentioned by chance the reflux from the previous day but thought it was nothing more than indigestion. He stopped me in mid-sentence and said we need to get that checked it sounds like Angina! I nearly burst out laughing *"But I'm in good shape, training regularly, I'm not overweight, I have never smoked, I eat well and only drink occasionally."* He insisted it sounded like classic symptoms and booked me an emergency appointment the following week at the Cardiovascular unit of St James' Hospital in Leeds. This was not what I was expecting. Physically and mentally, I was feeling really good and suddenly I was being tested for heart problems!

The tests did not go well. There were issues and they needed immediate attention. I was loaded with beta blockers and angina meds and sent home told to take it easy and to prepare for detailed tests followed by an angiogram. It seemed to me at that point, that my life was over. Angina? Heart medications? What about my family? What about my coaching career? What about going to the gym? In my mind no matter what happened it was the end. All the information I was given confirmed to me that I was finished in rugby and that life as I knew it was over. I suddenly felt vulnerable and mortal, what about the future? Would I have one? Ridiculously over reactive but it was the unknown and I was frightened, I hadn't ever considered this would happen to me.

Mentally I was a wreck. I remember sitting in a recovery room after the angiogram with lots of elderly and very ill-looking people and thought this is all a dream. I was only in my early fifties, I was, to all intents and purposes, as fit as a fiddle. I looked OK, I felt OK, what was I doing here? I had no family history of heart disease, I had normal blood pressure, yet I was having a procedure I associated with the old and very ill. I was struggling to come to terms with all of this. It was decided I needed stents and I was booked for an angioplasty the following week.

Half-way through the angioplasty, (a procedure that entails threading a tube into the blood vessels in your wrist and up into the main arteries of the heart where a stent is placed to increase the flow of blood), it stopped. The surgeons and assistants all left the theatre to discuss something with a Senior Consultant. I remember laying there for what seemed like hours, but was in fact 10 minutes, thinking they've realised there's nothing wrong and it's all been for nothing and I can go back to normal life. No such luck!

They had encountered some problems. The Senior Consultant had been called for a second opinion. Back in they came to tell me that it was too dangerous to continue and that the Consultant would see me back in recovery. Now, not only was I mentally in pieces I was genuinely frightened. It's amazing what goes through your mind when you start to try and guess what's going on and see only a negative outcome. My wife had been due to come and collect me later that day. The nurse in the recovery ward said that they had rung her to come down a little earlier so she could be there when the consultant came back to speak to me. More stress!!

It seems I suffer from Myositis Ossificans. When I played if I ever suffered from a dead leg or corked thigh instead of severe bruising I often ended up with a lump. Simply put it is when the muscle calcifies.

The Senior Consultant, who it transpired was a big Rugby fan, came to speak to me and laid out the findings. He had stopped the angioplasty because stents were not the answer to this problem and any attempt to continue could have had a catastrophic outcome. My arteries were calcifying i.e., turning to bone. One artery was completely closed, one was almost closed, and one was closing fast. I needed an urgent heart bypass. Now that just about finished me off. I couldn't get my head around this. I had just returned from a World Championship coaching a team to a Gold Medal, I was coaching on the world stage, feeling in great shape and being told this news was surreal.

Through the fog of emotions, I vaguely remember him saying that it is a major operation that has high risks, and he would give me six months, if I sat still. I thought he meant six months to decide whether to have the operation or not, but it was six months to live! I can honestly say that my first thought was that life was over. Even if I had the operation, I would be infirm and weak, I laugh now but I saw myself being pushed around in a wheelchair with a blanket tucked around my legs.

After delivering his news in a concise manner with no fluff, he asked for my first thoughts. I laughed nervously and said, *"I wish I had drunk all those beers and eaten all those chips I turned down trying to stay healthy"*.

"Let me tell you" he said, *"that is what has saved your life. Given the state of your arteries and the training regime you are partaking in you could have dropped dead at any moment. Only because your heart is in such good shape has it been able to work overtime and pump enough blood to keep you alive"*. He then explained what was to happen and more importantly what would follow. He was adamant my life would return to normal, he laughed when I asked if I would ever work again. He told me I could be back on light duties in around 10 weeks and certainly back in the gym in some way a few weeks after the operation.

On reflection Mr. Munsch, the Consultant was a perfect Head Coach. He knew his stuff; he was leader in his field. He had the vision. He told me what needed to be done and why and what could be achieved by doing this. He gave me detail and the big picture. Finally, he knew how to deal with such life changing news. I have said how distressed, frightened and unsure I was. My immediate thoughts were that I was finished with the life I was used to. With all his experience he was used to that. His manner and his message gave me a different outlook. Here was something that wouldn't derail me and that with the correct medication and lifestyle I would be back to normal in no time. His confidence was reassuring, his positive outlook was comforting. He laid out what was possible.

It wasn't a pleasant experience, the operation was long, with blood transfusions in the days following. Immediate recovery was uncomfortable and painful but 10 weeks later I was walking several miles across the Yorkshire Moors, attending the gym daily and excited once again at what life had in store!

DAMIAN MCGRATH

ONE SEAT TO THE RIGHT
PRESSURE

I loved being an assistant coach. Supporting the Head Coach, supporting the players, having a huge input into training and preparation. Being a sounding board for the Head Coach, giving opinions, challenging, sometimes playing devil's advocate and enjoying the success that might come with it.

As Assistant Coach at Leeds Rhinos, on game day I would sit next to the Head Coach in the middle of the main stand at the famous Headingly stadium. When the TV cameras panned up to the Coach's Box, there I was passing on messages from the Head Coach to the bench discussing possible substitutions and giving my thoughts when asked. It was always a fantastic feeling when you won and very disappointing when you lose just like in any sporting situation. However, despite doing this for several years sitting on the left-hand side of the head coach amidst crowds of 20,000 plus every other week enjoying the highs and lows of Super League I still had no inkling of what the real difference was between being the Assistant and being the Head Coach.

Midway through another successful season, the then Head Coach, Graham Murray, had to return to Australia upon the sudden death of his mother. He would be gone for two weeks. It was felt nothing needed to change; I would take over as Interim Head Coach in his short absence. The club's successes had given my personal standing a real boost, I had just been appointed as Assistant Coach to the National Team ahead of the upcoming World Cup. Allied to that the team we're on fantastic run of results, playing great rugby and the feeling in the squad was very positive. The two fixtures we would play during Graham's absence were against teams in the bottom four of Super League. Comfortable victories were expected.

For the first game at home a big crowd assembled and it was live on TV. I was excited, nervous but full of great anticipation. We had trained really well, I was happy with my last words in the changing room, the Friday night weather was perfect, the team was at full strength, confident and a strong performance was expected.

Within 15 minutes of the kick-off we were losing 20 points to nil. This wasn't in the script! This wasn't supposed to happen! Our game plan was in tatters. From an early air of disbelief, there was now outright agitation and mutterings from the large crowd. We were struggling to react to adversity, I had the feeling that 20,000 plus people had their eyes on me as well as the many watching at home on TV. Out of the corner of my eye, I saw my face flash on the big screen in the corner of the stadium. What to do? Shout? Scream? Panic? Make hasty decisions based on emotion?

At that moment I truly understood what pressure was, in a sporting context. It was moving one seat to the right. Now I wasn't giving an opinion I had to make decisions and it gave me a sharp reminder and a great insight into what being a leader really was. It wouldn't always be plain sailing. Dealing with the unexpected, being the person relied upon to make correct, insightful and positive decisions when things weren't going to plan. Having a plan-B, or just being a calming voice. Although I had been Head Coach at Academy and Reserve team level, I had never operated under such levels of scrutiny and the overwhelming desire to be seen to be doing something was as great as I had known it.

We came back strongly to win the game comfortably but more through the players efforts than mine. The following week was another TV game away at the bottom club. It was a famous RL club who were fighting for survival and despite their position had some very good players. We came back to scrape a win in a tight game. In the TV interview afterwards I had to admit I felt I'd aged considerably in just a couple of weeks. The lessons learned from that experience have stuck with me forever. Everybody has an opinion, everybody feels they can see the right way forward but the difference between giving an opinion and making a decision is a huge and when that decision has to be made under the critical gaze of an unforgiving crowd and a judgmental TV audience the pressure to act, as well as be right, is off the scale.

As well as the audience, I also learned of the pressure from players and most importantly from me. At half time in both fixtures, the players, World Class players no less, looked to me for answers, for validation and for belief. Experience allows you to be ready for these times. If you don't know what to say and how to say it, you undermine your credibility instantly. On a personal level I reviewed my actions, thoughts and words during those two weeks. I was, on reflection, putting huge pressure on myself. Trying to match up against the highly experienced 'master coach' who I was standing in for. When things didn't quite go to plan, I instantly worried about how people would view me and judge me rather than thinking about the team and the game.

The pressure to be successful becomes greater as you progress as a leader/coach. But dealing with it can become easier. It has to be planned for. Having a 'what if' checklist prepared for any possible scenario and instance. Even if it doesn't bring victory or success you will not have that feeling that you could have done more.

AUSTRALIA

Just like every Rugby Union fan looks forward to the British and Irish Lions tours, for Rugby League fans the arrival of the touring Kangaroos every four years was a time to savour.

The stars of Australian rugby could only be read about or, if you were lucky, glimpsed on a videocassette that was sent from Down Under. To see them in action you had to watch them on the tours and fans always flocked to see them. In 1986 the Kangaroos went unbeaten; they became known as The Invincibles. At that time, I was teaching at Shakespeare Middle school in Leeds and the Aussies often trained on a company sports field directly opposite the school. If the weather was fine, I would find any excuse to take my class outside and we would sit and watch them train. The girls of course weren't interested, but for the boys and me it was a chance to get up close and see these giants of the game preparing. That team was full of some of the greatest players of all time, Wally Lewis, Peter Sterling and Mal Meninga among them.

Fast forward a few years and I was called up to RLHQ and asked if I could help out with a voluntary role for three weeks. The Rugby League World Cup Final was being held at Wembley in 1992. After a long and protracted qualification process. Great Britain would be up against the all-conquering Australians. Australia were flying in and would be based in Leeds for two weeks. They would play a warm up game, then travel to London for the final. Could I act as their liaison officer? As an aspiring young coach this was a lottery win. I was contacted by the Australian Rugby League and given an outline-training schedule. I had to source some quality training venues, liaise with the hotel and coach firm and generally make myself available to the team.

Now I felt my coach education was beginning. I was welcomed

into the group with no issues. I got access to all their training sessions, travelled on the team coach to training and the warm-up games but best of all I got to sit and spend time with the coaching staff and the players. There were no mobile phones, no play stations, no heavy press intrusions just a few beers and stories. I sat and listened and savoured every second. The Head Coach was Bob Fulton, one of the games most famous players and the Team Manager was Geoff Carr, one the ARL's most senior administrators. I became great friends with the Strength & Conditioner, Shaun McRae, and Assistant Coach, Frank Ponissi. Shaun was S&C at the Canberra Raiders, who at that time were the dominant team in Australia and Frank was assistant to Fulton at Manly RL. I mention their names because over the next three or four years they helped catapult my learning and experience beyond my wildest dreams.

In 1994 the Kangaroos returned on their big tour to Britain and France. Once more the same staff were leading the tour and this time, they requested that the RFL appoint me as their liaison officer. I was given leave by the ever-supportive Leeds City council to work the tour and so began a learning experience money can't buy. The team trained twice a day and armed with a notebook and pen I documented it all. I attended rehabilitation sessions with the medical staff, I travelled with the team to and from games, sometimes, where space allowed, I had dressing room access, it was gold dust. They were streets ahead of us in preparation, in feedback, in game plans and attitude. But once again the real value was the socialising. I felt more comfortable with the group and more accepted, as I wasn't new on the scene. I asked about the thought process behind training, what was the key factor behind their dominance? Everything was 'How', 'what' or 'Why'. Their patience with me was admirable. Any sports fixture now is preceded by a warm-up. Some of them, in rugby in particular, are as lengthy and more complicated as any game! It was the first time I had ever seen a team warm-up, before a game it was basic, short and sweet but new and groundbreaking. It's hard to imagine that now but they explained the rationale and it made sense. Shaun and Frank led most of the training and they opened my eyes to skills drills and how and why they fit in a session. They used them imaginatively in warm-ups and warm-downs, they had different practices for injured players, different sessions for the players who were fit but not selected for certain games, all of these things we take for granted now but back then, for us, it was normally one size fits all. I watched Fulton introduce his game plan in scenarios and feedback sessions and then construct training sessions around them. It seems strange as I write this now and recall those days but the use of the ball in fitness drills and bags and shields in defensive drills was something completely new.

The touring group was once again full of some of the games greatest ever players, some competing for the same position so it was particularly interesting to see how the coach handled the group and dealt with all the egos and cliques. One evening I sat with Bob and Geoff and over a beer talked just about coaching. The importance of team leaders and communicating the plan was the message. I wanted to know how he dealt with non-selected players. He told me he picked the team but always gave each player the reason they weren't selected. He said they will never agree with you but at least they know you have a reason and it's not personal. He talked about the importance of being consistent with your message, don't say one thing and do another, and one that stuck out was, select the leaders early, the influencers he called them, and use them to drive the team forward on and off the field. That one has always stuck with me and been one of the best pieces of advice I ever received.

Everything I have just mentioned should be second nature to most coaches yet what we discussed and what I saw in action was completely new and eye opening.

On reflection my favourite part was usually over meals or a drink in the bar listening to stories and discussing coaching and preparation. This is where Bob Fulton's advice was dispensed. *"Don't stand still because the game doesn't"* was a gem he mentioned often. I remember driving him to a function and he was asking about my coaching ambitions. He listened and said, *"Would you like a job like mine?"* I laughed and said *"What, coach the best players in the world?, who wouldn't?"* His reply has stuck with me. *"Mate, don't let your ambition and your ability get mixed up"*. He talked about the value of experience and not to run before you could walk. *"Find somewhere that is out of the spotlight and make mistakes. Too many people take positions they aren't ready for. They are good coaches but don't have the back story to help then navigate the hard times and deal properly with the good times."*

One last thing that stays in my mind was a conversation about my coaching. I told him how much of an upturn there had been in my coaching once I became more collaborative and used the people around me as sounding boards. He said *"The biggest mistake I see with Head Coaches is surrounding themselves with their mates. They just get 'yes' men, who are no threat to their position. I only look to appoint the best I can in every role. These people challenge you and make you think. They can give a different perspective. Always encourage their opinions, make them feel valued and you and the team will be successful."* All these years later it still proves to be sound advice.

The following year, 1995 the RL World Cup was being held in the UK. It developed into an exciting and thrilling competition. Great Britain split to play as England and Wales alongside Australia, NZ, Samoa, Ireland, Fiji, Tonga, PNG, France and South Africa. The Pacific Island teams were packed with Australian NRL players and Wales were full of extremely talented ex Rugby Union stars such as Jonathan Davies. I was contacted in good time by the ARL to be their liaison. The touring staff were the same guys (bar one) I had worked with before and to say I was excited about the prospect was an understatement. This time the three weeks were going to be a little different. I was to be with the team full time and stay in the hotel. Before I had always slept at home as I was local. I was given a full kit allocation, which was very welcome but different from before when I was given a couple of t-shirts etc. I just thought it was because I was a regular over the last few years and had built up a great relationship with the team so thought nothing of it.

The reason soon became clear; war was being waged for Rugby League. In one corner was the Australian Rugby League (ARL) who ran the game and were supported by Media mogul, Kerry Packer, (who had revolutionised cricket with a breakaway competition 20 years previously) and in the other corner, Rupert Murdoch, and his planned Super League breakaway. At this point the players and clubs, particularly in Australia, were being wooed by both sides and asked to choose. Those that sided with the ARL, the governing body, were eligible for selection, the others were not considered and that included S&C Shaun McRae, whose club Canberra Raiders, had opted for Super League. It was a real mess and was getting nasty.

So, when the team arrived it took on almost a siege mentality and they pulled up the drawbridge so to speak. Hence the reason for my becoming a permanent part of the group. The politics raged over months to come but for now I really got to see the team operate up close. I listened in on selection I travelled as part of the team to all games, even on the coach to the final! I was in the dressing room I listened to team talks and even did some basic stats during the games. Now of course there are no mystical rituals that successful people or teams undertake and what I had underlined was the simplicity of their approach in selection, tactics, substitution rationale, team talks, half time organisation, feedback and training. Everything was planned and thought through, and everyone, players and staff knew "why"! But when asked by friends afterwards what stood out it was the consistency. Consistency of message, consistency of standards and, the thing that all top players have, the ability to do the little things consistently well.

After the 1995 World Cup my own coaching circumstances were changing for the better as my senior career began to take off and so I sadly had to step down from anymore liaison work, but a by-product of my close relationship with the coaches and administration staff had been an invitation the previous year to come to Australia and spend time at some of the leading clubs. How could I resist that chance?

It was my first time to Australia; in fact, apart from one brief trip to the USA, it was my first time out of Europe. I had no idea how far it was and just how big Australia was. The in-flight entertainment was one large TV screen, that showed a movie that you either watched or didn't. In between the screen displayed the flight path on a map of the world. I remember clearly seeing that the plane was travelling over the north coast of Australia, from the look of the map we were only a small distance from Sydney. I put my seat back upright, put my table up, put my book in my bag in the overhead locker, checked my seat belt was fastened and prepared for landing. I thought I was getting some strange looks as I did it and when we finally landed around four or five hours later, I understood why – it is a big country! Just to compound my misery and truly underline my naivety I was travelling in t-shirt and shorts; well, it was June and I was going to Australia where it is hot – isn't it? Of course, June in the southern hemisphere is mid winter, the temperature was one degree and bloody freezing. God knows what people were thinking as I shivered my way through customs. You live and learn!

My first stop was Canberra, the home of the 'Green Machine', the Canberra Raiders. They were at the time, along with the Brisbane Broncos, the pre-eminent team in the Australian Rugby League. The team contained many of the stars of the Australian National team who I had got to meet on the Kangaroo tours. Shaun McRae picked me up and I dived straight in to life at the Raiders. I was afforded almost full access to everything that went on behind the scenes. I had dressing room access on game days, watched the games from the coach's box but most of all was given time by people who really didn't have to do it. I was used to the closed shop of British RL where people kept what they did a guarded secret. Training and tactics for instance were not for public consumption. This was almost the opposite. Head Coach, Tim Sheens, was and still is regarded as one of the great thinkers as well as one of the most successful RL coaches. He made time on several occasions to talk with me and explain his thinking. He answered all my questions and posed questions to me that made me think. What stood out then, and I still remember now, is that despite the huge gulf in our standing in the game, he questioned me on many things in British RL, he was curious and interested in training methods, in rugby philosophies and innovations, a trait I have noticed in all successful coaches. A coach is usually measured on the trophies he wins. Tim Sheens certainly doesn't fall short on that score, but its his influence on others that I think should not be forgotten. Many of his staff and players went on to great things themselves in the senior coaching arena.

Shaun McRae came to the UK and led St Helens to Super League and Challenge Cup success, before returning to Coach South Sydney in the NRL. Reserve team coach, Dean Lance, also came to England to coach Leeds Rhinos. From the players, Craig Bellamy is arguably one of the games most successful coaches ever, leading the Melbourne Storm to numerous finals. Mal Meninga coached the Raiders, Queensland State of Origin as well as the Kangaroos to a 2017 World Cup win. Ricky Stuart coaches in the NRL and has coached State of Origin and the Australian national team. That is far from an exhaustive list but the influence of the innovative and deep-thinking coach stretches far and wide.

DAMIAN MCGRATH

PATIENCE

In the introduction I alluded to the many self-help titles available. There is, it seems, a blueprint for everything from buying a house, to downloading movies, to losing weight.

But for things like illness, death, divorce and debt for instance there isn't one, you have to go through the process and experience it to have any idea how to deal with it. Success is in the same category, there is no manual, just know-how that comes from experience and patience.

Patience we are told is a virtue, a behaviour we must all show at so many points in our daily life. Yet it is often sacrificed in the clamour to be better, to be a winner. The trial and error of what does and doesn't work is often long and too often deflating but so is working with teams and individuals. It is rare to achieve big changes instantly and although that can and does happen, usually it is time that is needed for success or improvement to occur. It needs patience.

Building a successful career often takes time and effort. It requires patience to develop new skills, gain experience, and climb the ladder, It takes time to acquire new knowledge and skills, and patience allows you to embrace the learning process without becoming overwhelmed or discouraged. By being patient, you give yourself the opportunity to grow and stay relevant in a rapidly evolving world. Patience is valuable in building and maintaining professional relationships. Collaborating with colleagues, players and stakeholders often requires understanding their perspectives, actively listening, and resolving conflicts. Patience allows you to navigate challenging situations with diplomacy, empathy, and open-mindedness, fostering stronger connections and enabling effective teamwork. It contributes to effective decision-making and problem-solving in your career. Rushing into decisions without careful consideration can lead to mistakes or missed opportunities. Patience gives you the space to gather relevant information, weigh options, and analyse potential outcomes before making a well-informed choice. It also helps you approach problems with a calm and methodical mindset, enhancing your ability to find creative solutions.

At the beginning my coaching life I was keen to get where I was going. I felt I had all the answers. If ever there was an embodiment of someone who wanted to run before he could walk, I was it! Hindsight is a wonderful thing but I am far better equipped now than I was then. The American entertainer, Eddie Cantor, famously said *"It took me 30 years to be an overnight success."*

Many years ago, I was told about Chinese Bamboo. Bamboo is such an important and versatile plant. Its uses range from fuel, food, construction, clothing and kitchenware, to writing implements, musical instruments, furniture and weapons. To get the benefit of all these things however takes time. It takes a bamboo tree on average five years to grow. The first four years or so it cannot be seen, it's in the ground. However, it is still watered and nurtured every day even though there is no discernible change. But then in the space of five weeks it shoots up over 90 feet tall. Without prior knowledge you could be mistaken for thinking that Bamboo is the equivalent of an overnight success. Arriving from nowhere in spectacular fashion but in reality, it's taken several years of careful and deliberate preparation. The outcome is recognised but the journey with its sacrifices and commitment is generally ignored. Yet it is the part that makes the difference.

Having a vision; it is vital to understand what you want to see as the desired outcome. Understanding your subject gives you the knowledge to make it happen and your personality gives you the patience to see the journey through.

THE DOUBT PERCENTAGE

*Just before we broke up for the Christmas holidays, I asked the class
I was teaching a question, "Would you like a treat"?*

If they did, I said they needed to put their hands up as high as they
could. A forest of arms went up searching for the sky! *"Ok"*, I said,
*"but if you put them even higher, we will watch a film instead of doing
our normal lessons"*. Amazingly they all found a few more inches,
their shoulders nearly coming out of their sockets to demonstrate
how much they wanted to do it. At that moment I discovered what I
call 'The Doubt Percentage'.

No matter how eloquent, persuasive or inspirational we may be
when we lay out our vision, it's never quite enough. If you've done it
well your team or group will set about the process with gusto. But
whether they realise it or not they have more to give. As the vision
becomes a reality, they find those hidden depths because they can
see the worth in extending themselves even more than they thought
possible. They just needed a reason to push harder, to give absolutely
all they've got.

Everybody can push a few inches higher if its something they
want, something they think is worth the effort. It is a phenomenon I
have seen repeated over and over again.

I took over as Head Coach of Germany Rugby Sevens in 2019.
Although rugby is a niche sport in a football mad country, they
were blessed with a small but naturally talented group. They had
prominence in world circles but had never achieved the next step up
into the Elite levels of the World Series etc. They had a reputation
as 'nearly men', coming close to success but not quite making it. As
you might expect I did my due diligence. I studied their players,

their style of play and compiled my own SWOT list. (Strengths, Weaknesses, Opportunities, Threats).

From my observations it was obvious there was a talented core of players. They had skill and they some game understanding. On the down side there was no genuine speed or size in the team, which when compared to the elite sides was a major weakness. I saw a big opportunity to harness their togetherness and play a style which I felt would overcome their perceived weaknesses and make them stronger. The threat to my plan was two-fold.

Firstly, would my plan work against the opposition we would meet, but crucially could I persuade them to abandon their current approach for the one that in my opinion suited them more? Of course, in sport, like much of life, it's all about opinions. I was certain that the way they currently played did not suit them. It was all they knew, and was modelled on one of the world's most successful teams but I felt they didn't have the personnel to pull it off properly.

I laid out my vision, told them what I felt we could achieve, what we needed to do, why we should do it and the benefits. I stressed the hard work that would be required in terms of fitness and they would have to allow me to teach them what they thought they already knew, (basic skills).

They were, and they remain, a fantastic group of young men. I couldn't fault their attitude, but it is always difficult changing. As well as the field I used the classroom as much as possible. No one reacts well to being told they're doing it wrong or that their efforts haven't produced the best results. I tried to blend footage of the style I thought would suit them with similar situations from their previous games. I tried to prove my point in as positive a way as possible. They were a smart bunch, they accepted many of my points and began to push hard in training, but they struggled with fitness and consistency. At the end of the first training block, I presented each player with a postcard on which I wrote some brief personal feedback. At the bottom of each one I wrote the same thing; *"Nichts ist unmöglich!"* – Nothing is impossible! I knew that they were finding it difficult and I was privately a little disappointed with progress despite their efforts. However, experience had taught me that persistence would pay off, if we had patience and worked as hard as we possibly could.

I went for a coffee with the leadership group, we talked about what was happening and I sought their opinions. They supported what we were doing and they felt it would help bring them sustained success but they weren't sure they could pull it off. Their feeling was they were trying as hard as they could to play with this new approach but didn't think it was happening. I showed them some KPIs (key performance indicators) I had been using to measure improvement. Each week of the training block I had asked our analyst to measure certain metrics that I felt were important if we were to achieve our aims. The weekly measurements indicated significant week on week improvements, we were getting there even if it felt like no progress was being made. I shared them with the leaders who were visibly surprised but ultimately delighted by the story the numbers told. They asked if I would share them with the whole squad. Although numbers don't always tell a full story and statistics can be manipulated, these numbers had an invigorating effect. The Doubt Percentage had been affecting us, because buoyed by my revelations, training intensity increased and the enthusiasm in the group was noticeably higher. I even heard the captain telling the team when they were in their huddle at the end of a session to stay focused because *"Nichts war unmöglich!"* – Nothing was impossible!

DAMIAN MCGRATH

BRAVERY

If you had to list the attributes required to be a coach or a leader how many of you would include bravery in that list?

To most people bravery is associated with war or conflict but coaches and leaders are courageous people. They are prepared to take on responsibility and open themselves up to intense scrutiny.

On a personal level it meant I had to step outside of my comfort zone, confront my fears, and take bold actions to achieve my goals. But for all coaches it involves having the courage to face challenges, take risks, and make difficult decisions in pursuit of success. You need the resilience to bounce back from adversity, and the mental fortitude to perform at your best under pressure. It may seem easy to try new strategies, introduce innovative techniques, or make a bold team selection, but the chance of criticism or even ridicule is always there. For the fainthearted it may seem safer to just do enough and take the tried and tested option but a good coach will have the confidence to push their boundaries to perform at their best even under the most challenging of circumstances.

Until I began to write this, I had never thought of myself as brave, but in this context, I am, and continue to be, a brave man. I chronicle elsewhere my crushing shyness and lack of confidence, yet I still pursued a career, first in teaching, then coaching that necessitated me standing up in front of people and confronting my worst fears. However, my bravest act was yet to come. It is a sad fact of sporting life in much of English sport that coaches are often given opportunities based on their playing prowess and coaches without a high-profile playing career are judged in a somewhat lesser light. But it isn't an insurmountable obstacle, I suppose it depends on how much you want it. I have met many coaches who complain about the lack of opportunities for those of us who aren't perhaps well known enough to be considered automatically for coaching roles, but how badly do you want to do it? Does it have to be geographically or financially acceptable? Does it need security attached or are you prepared to take a chance, even move backwards to move forwards in the future? At Leeds I was offered my dream job as Assistant First Team coach right off the bat, but I asked if I could head up the Academy instead. Was that a brave move? Maybe I would never get the chance again? Or was stepping back to the Academy a smart play? I certainly thought so. I knew I wasn't ready to work with the calibre of players in the senior team but I knew I could and would make my mark with the talented youngsters in the Academy. Many of my friends saw it as a backwards step but I knew it was step back that would take me forward. Coaching isn't a linear progression how many people are brave enough to move sideways or backwards to find a way forwards?

As I began my professional coaching career, I looked to grab every opportunity that came my way. I had a day job to begin with and my roles at first, Batley RLFC as Reserve team coach, then as Head of Academy at Leeds paid no more than a couple of thousand pounds a year (it just about covered petrol), but necessitated a lot of time, not only in training and playing, but preparation. Family time was squeezed but I had belief in my ability and knew that to have any hope of progressing further up the ladder I had to prove myself however I could, and try and make myself indispensable. When the opportunity came to become full time Assistant First Team Coach at Leeds Rhinos Rugby League it was the chance I had worked so hard for, but the choice wasn't easy. It was less money than I was making in the job I had and I would have to abandon the security and pension it gave me. But it was what I wanted to do and I saw it as a great opportunity. I took the job determined to make it work. It was a successful time but a change of Head Coach in 2000 saw my resilience firmly tested as he brought in his own people and I was out of a job.

At that time London Broncos were under the new ownership of

Sir Richard Branson, he wanted to establish top level Rugby League in the capital and had invested heavily in the team, bringing over a multitude of high-profile Australian and New Zealand Rugby League stars. For their new coach, Tony Rea, it was his first coaching role and he was looking for an experienced assistant, we met and chatted and he offered me the job. It was an exciting role. I would be able to work with some of the world's best players, test myself at their level and I knew the experience would be hard to match. Straightforward it would seem but I was a married man with three young children, the pay was no better than my previous role, we couldn't afford to all move down. The children were in school, my wife was working. If I turned it down the dream would essentially be over. Choice and chance raised its head again. We decided we had come too far and sacrificed too much to give in. I took the job and moved away from home and everyone I knew for the first time! It seems crazy now but moving to London then felt like moving countries, my support network was four or five hours up the M1 motorway but I was sure this was the step I needed to take to move forward.

I spent a year at the Broncos. The team was almost entirely made up of Aussies and Kiwis, including the respective captains of each country as well as many other full internationals. It was a great environment, professionally I was questioned and challenged on a daily basis, I was made to think about training in a different way, I was exposed to tactical nuances I hadn't considered and best of all I learned something new everyday. As an added bonus I got to work with two great practitioners. Head Coach, Tony Rea, was a smart operator, he knew the game but knew he didn't have all the answers. He was always looking to make things better and gave me plenty of opportunities to lead training. Head of Strength and Conditioning was a true great of British Sport, Kelvin Giles. As well as being one time Head Coach of UK Athletics he had held a similar role for the Australian Institute of Sport and had been Head of Performance for the Brisbane Broncos in the NRL for several years as they dominated the game. Working closely with Kelvin and having the opportunity to question and observe him in action is something I regard as a career highlight. Despite the struggle of being away from home and the family I loved every minute of my time in London. The staff and players made coming to work everyday a real pleasure.

However, I couldn't see a way forward as a coach in Rugby League. The barriers to someone like me getting a Head Coach role seemed as large as ever, I was ambitious, I was keen and I felt like I was treading water. I had worked my way up the ladder from the Academy to the Senior team and held similar roles with the National teams but I knew that the next step as a Head Coach in Super League would remain out of reach.

At that time Rugby Union as a professional sport was in its infancy, the game was trying to find its identity. Under Clive Woodward, the England National team was making its mark. Clive had embraced professionalism and surrounded himself with a group of talented coaches. One of these was Phil Larder, a man I knew very well from his Rugby League days. Phil had been Head of Coach Development at the RFL as well as Coaching Great Britain and a couple of Super League sides. I saw the impact that he was making using his league knowledge and skills. As England's defence coach he was changing the face of the game. He wasn't the only convert. Two of Rugby League's all time great players had joined him. Ellery Hanley was defence coach for the England 'A' team set up and my good friend Joe Lydon had moved from being the RFL's Performance Director to head up the newly formed Rugby Sevens programme that would compete on the World series. I spoke often to Joe about how he was finding life in what was a different sport. I was intrigued by how he saw the chance to make an impact on how the game was played and how players could develop.

As the season with the Broncos came to a close Joe informed me of a possible opportunity in the England RFU national set up. Ellery Hanley had left his position and there was an opening in a dual role, as England 'A' Defence and Skills Coach and to be Assistant Coach to Joe with England Sevens. Now when I mentioned bravery earlier it is this sort of moment I particularly had in mind. I don't mind admitting that I was incredibly excited by what may lay ahead, I was confident I could make a real impact in Rugby Union both in attack and defence. The fact that the sport was played across the world only added to the possibilities. However, it was by no means a straightforward decision. I would be entering the unknown, I had no background in the sport, no connections. My life had been all Rugby League up to this point, it was a life I was comfortable in. I wouldn't be joining Rugby Union as a big name convert unlike the others I have mentioned, I would have to fight to make my mark and establish myself as a coach with a lot to offer. Whilst this was a big decision, I decided now was the time to do it, it was a chance to move forward and explore new horizons. That part was relatively easy, the real stumbling block was money. The RFU's budget was set and wouldn't change for a few months, they wanted to see how I got on and make sure I was the right man for the job. The offer was to be reviewed after a set period. It was less than half my present salary with the Broncos. Now let me say that money has never been my motivator but this would put a huge strain on the family and I as much as I wanted to do it, I knew it was going to be difficult to justify. There was no guarantee that I would succeed and I could find myself out on my ear with no job at all. The easy choice or the brave one? Play it safe or back myself? My wife knew how much of our lives had been invested in my journey and she supported me 100%. I jumped in and took the chance offered!

I have told these anecdotes to give an example of just how brave you have to be with your choices if you want to progress. But also, to illustrate that your journey isn't always a straight line in an upwards direction. Both financially, geographically and in the type of role you take, sometimes it may be a step back to go forward.

How brave are you?

CHECK YOUR JUNK MAIL BEFORE YOU DELETE IT

After being lured back from Wales to England Sevens, my future suddenly looked grim once again. The promised opportunities didn't materialise, and after an eventful 16 months the scrap heap was once again beckoning. I was informed that due to changes there was now no position for me.

I am without a shadow of a doubt a glass half-full person, I always look forward and even in low moments I look to press on regardless. But this time I was already at a low point after the heart bypass had floored me physically and mentally. This treatment by the England RFU had no regard for my personal well being or the promises that had been made.

I really felt let down and couldn't see any way forward. Quite by chance I met my old friend and colleague, Terry Sands. Terry was the owner of Samurai Sports and we had worked together with England 'A' and England Sevens in the past. Terry was also Rugby Chairman at Bury St Edmonds RUFC down in Suffolk. He knew of my circumstances and offered me some part-time work at the club a couple of days a week as a Skills and Defence Coach. It was a long old trip from Leeds to the east coast, but the club organised me a room and use of a vehicle, I was back in the game albeit in a limited way but very happy. The travelling was a bind, but the club and players made it all worthwhile.

A couple weeks into the role I happened to look on Facebook and came across a conversation discussing an advert for a rugby job that was being advertised. I clicked on the link and it was from the Samoan Rugby Union. They wanted a new Head Coach for their Sevens programme. For those that aren't familiar with rugby, Samoa, despite its size, is a rugby stronghold. It boasts a rich heritage and many famous names have represented Manu Samoa over the years. In 2009 Samoa Sevens were the Rugby World Series Champions. They had a golden crop of players who had brought great success to this proud, rugby mad, tiny island. But now six years later they were in decline. No Cup Final appearances for several years never coming close to the World title again. A succession of coaches were sacked, there was constant political interference and a demanding public. They took the momentous decision, in Samoan eyes, to consider an overseas coach for the very first time for their flagship rugby programme.

What did I have to lose? I emailed my CV and a cover letter, not really expecting anything to happen. It was one of many job applications I sent out, admittedly more in hope than anything. I heard nothing and to be quite truthful I had forgotten all about it!

Several weeks later I was sat down in Bury St Edmonds, browsing social media and the internet, for no other reason that I had nothing else to do. I checked my emails for the millionth time and decided to tidy up my 'Inbox'. I then opened my junk folder which had almost a hundred emails in. I don't know about you, but I usually just clicked the box that highlighted them all and pressed delete. But for some reason, probably because I had time to kill, I looked to see what they were and deleted them one by one.

There it was! Half-way down the page was an email from the Samoan Rugby Union Secretary, Matafeo George Latu. I nearly missed it!!

Dear Damian you have been shortlisted for an interview by the selection panel by teleconference for the above position on Friday the 24 July 2015 at 8.30 am local time. I understand we have a 12 hour time difference between the UK and Samoa. Please find out what time it will be from your end then we can make the arrangements for hook up. rgds

Matafeo George Latu
Secretary I Samoa Rugby Union

So almost 11 weeks after sending in my application I had an interview. It was for 9.30pm the following evening! I confirmed it instantly, then contacted Terry Sands. I had to find somewhere to take the call. Sandsy organised for me to sit in the clubhouse bar and use the club telephone. He said he would wait for me to finish – Neither of us had any idea it would take so long.

The phone rang just after 9.40pm, introductions were made, the interview format was explained and off we went. Two things almost beat me from the off. First of all, the connection from that tiny island in the South Pacific was temperamental and secondly my ears. Some of the accents of the interviewers were difficult to pick up. Not only were they speaking in heavily accented English, for my benefit, but it was difficult to pick up on a telephone line that sounded as though it was two tin cans connected by a piece of string!

Half-way through the first question being asked the line went dead. They redialled and we went again. About five minutes into the interview, I launched into a long and detailed answer to a particular question, I finished, felt really pleased with my answer and… silence. The line had dropped again. They called back; sorry could I repeat the answer. It was a blow; I wasn't sure I could match the passion and enthusiasm I had poured into my first attempt. We carried on in the same vein throughout the whole interview, a question followed by what I hoped were great answers and more often than not deafening silence before a call back and a request to repeat my answer. Well over two and a half hours later we finished. The patience of the Samoan panel and their willingness to finish what we started was amazing, I'm not sure I could have persevered. I was mentally shot. The stress of an interview is one thing, repeating yourself continuously is another. It reminded me that bullshit doesn't always work – its hard to repeat it on a regular basis so I was glad I stuck to facts. I was tired but I got in the car for the five-hour drive back to Leeds. I was unsure how it had gone. On reflection I was really pleased with my answers and how I had dealt with all the distractions. But of course, I did not know how it had been received. I couldn't see anyone, no way of reading their reactions to me or my answers. However, I felt

I'd given it my best shot and consoled myself with the thought that I had at least been shortlisted for such a prestigious rugby role.

A couple of weeks went by with no communication, not even a polite rejection email. As you might expect I thought the post was filled and put it to the back of my mind. A byproduct of the experience was to always check your junk mail and I did it on a daily basis.

Which again was a good job because I received this:

Damian we are about to make an announcement on the Sevens position and we are making final background checks on those shortlisted. We note you have not included referees in your application. Can you provide names and contact details of any referees in particular your recent involvement with the English 7s. rgds

Matafeo George Latu
Secretary | Samoa Rugby Union

Because they hadn't asked for them, I hadn't included any in my original application. Now began a scramble not just to get the two guys I knew wouldn't hesitate to be my referees, but to make sure they would answer an overseas phone call from a number they didn't recognise. I contacted my great friends, England's Rugby Sevens Head Coach Simon Amor and USA Sevens Head Coach, Mike Friday. Both have strong reputations in Rugby Sevens, and both were keen to help. I had no idea if the reference request was a good sign or if everyone involved was being reference checked. On Friday August 7th I sat at home having a coffee thinking about the fourteen weeks that had passed since chancing on the job advertisement on Facebook of all places. I was constantly checking my emails, including Junk, every few minutes. Nothing, no news one way or another. Or so I thought. In my Inbox and Junk emails I had looked for George Latu's name but missed one sent from his wife's account!

Dear Damian,

George Latu here using my wife Brenda's iPad. The executive Board of the Samoa Rugby Union met this evening and I am pleased to advise you have resolved to offer you the position of Coach of the National 7's Team subject to the negotiation of the terms and conditions of your Contract with SRU.

You were the top candidate in a field of 29 of which 8 applicants were shortlisted for interview by an independent panel chaired by one of Samoa's leading private Consultants. The applicants came from 6 countries (including 3 from the UK) and were a highly experienced group of international and local coaches. The SRU CEO Vincent Fepuleai is copied and he will be in contact with you shortly. Would appreciate if you would keep this confidential until the SRU makes a formal announcement.

Regards George

What a rollercoaster. I was now the Head Coach of the Manu Samoa Sevens. Nine months after a heart bypass that I thought had ended my coaching career and life as I had known it, I was back at the sharp end and elated. I remember telling my friends months later that nothing is done overly quickly in that part of the world and the circumstances of my appointment should have prepared me for what was to come.

A "Palagi" (pronounced palangi) is the Samoan word for a white person or foreigner. This Palagi arrived and had no idea what to expect. I was excited about the possible talent pool available but unsure about everything else. I had done two telephone interviews prior to my arrival with radio stations in Australia and New Zealand, both were keen to know how I would deal with interference of the Prime Minister of Samoa who was also the Chairman of the Samoan Rugby Union, a man known to influence selection and be ruthless in disposing of coaches who didn't succeed. I was forewarned it, wouldn't be straightforward!

DAMIAN MCGRATH

SAMOA

*Now when it comes to pressure, nothing could have prepared me
for what I experienced in Samoa. I had learnt hard lessons from
my days at the Rhinos about the controllable pressures and how the
experienced coach operates.*

This was on a different level. In 2015 I was appointed as Head Coach
of the Manu Samoa Sevens team. It was not only a huge honour
for me but a momentous day in Samoan Rugby history. I was the
first non-Samoan to be appointed as a Head Coach of this famous
Rugby nation. I was a 'Palagi' (white man) brought in to revive
the rugby fortunes of this proud Pacific nation. Despite having a
reputation as one of the leading rugby nations many people have
no idea how small Samoa is. It consists of two little islands in the
Pacific. It only has a population of approximately 200,000 people.
The bulk of the people live on the smaller of the two islands, Upulo.
Samoa is without question paradise on earth. A beautiful place
with wonderful smiling people. A place of palm trees, white sands,
coconuts, an abundance of fresh fruit, non-stop sunshine and clear
blue sea. It is also a place where Rugby is King. I was told before I
arrived that there were three important things in a Samoan's life:
God, Family and Rugby. I soon found out the one thing that ignited
everyone's passion was Rugby. And I mean everybody.

Nothing could have prepared me for what I encountered. It
seemed not everyone was in favour of a Palagi (pronounced Palangi)
coach. The social media I read made that very clear. It wasn't just that
I was a foreigner, I was a foreigner most people had never heard of.

I also stepped into a one-party state. The Prime Minister who,
to all intents and purposes, ran a dictatorship, was also Chairman
of the Rugby Union and was known to make his thoughts and
wishes clear to everyone involved. During my time there he would

come to the gym most mornings with his security detail, sit on the exercise bike and watch the team lift weights. He never spoke to me or the players, but he was always an unsettling presence. One of the reasons an overseas coach was appointed was because of previous political interference. There had been a revolving door of coaches and players appointed and selected for personal gain by directors of the board and MPs alike. Being in a position of influence in the Samoan Rugby Union gave people great standing in the community and many liked to wield that influence for personal gain. Within the first few days it was clear that there were quite a few individuals who wanted to continue to pull the strings. I had emails from Ministers in Parliament about who should and shouldn't play before I'd met any players!!

Of the 200,000 people living in Samoa, at least 199,999 of them were expert coaches!!! Everyone, I would soon find out, had an opinion and they were never slow to tell me whenever they got chance. In shops, in restaurants, in bars/cafes, at traffic lights. If they couldn't tell me, they would let my wife know. I attended mass every Sunday at the huge Catholic Cathedral on Apia's waterfront. It wasn't unusual for the priest to wish me luck or encourage the players to train hard. I had some hilarious trips into town where at every traffic light or intersection I stopped at, someone would come the car window to offer some pearls of wisdom.

Rugby dominated TV and print media. TV news bulletins always had a rugby segment and there were sports shows in the evening that focussed purely on rugby it seemed. In the newspaper (there was only one and everyone read it) rugby was back-page and front-page news and depending on results, would often have a hard hitting editorial either lauding or decrying the team and its coach. It didn't help that I was probably the only person on the island with white hair, it meant I couldn't quietly blend in, escape was difficult. Samoa is an idyllic place from an outsider's point of view, but many locals live on the poverty line and life expectancy is considerably less than we are used to. Just like most of the other Pacific islands, many Samoans leave and go overseas to New Zealand and Australia for a better life.

They never lose their love for their beloved homeland and as well as sending money home they support their national rugby team with an even greater fervour. This is very evident on social media. Many despair, at the perceived corruption in the Rugby Union but still feel their team should beat everyone. There was no context in defeat – injuries, referee, bad luck, strength of opponents meant little, losing was a disaster, but winning was wonderful and nothing more than should be expected. I inherited a struggling group of players. There was little in the way of facilities and equipment but it was evident there was more than enough individual talent to create a team.

Spotting it was easy, the big challenge was creating a winning team in a culture that I didn't fully understand and under the unforgiving glare of a country that demanded and expected success.

DAMIAN MCGRATH

COMMUNICATION
IS IT MORE THAN WORDS?

I was sat one morning on a hotel veranda overlooking the bay in San Antonio, Ibiza. It was already hot, most sensible people were relaxing in the shade and the locals were going about their daily business before the heat was at its highest.

It was the 1980's I was on holiday with my pals. Despite a late finish the previous night we were up early to go on an organised excursion. One of the lads decided he wanted to buy an English newspaper and set off to find a shop that sold them. It wouldn't be an easy task as we were staying in, what was at that time, a mainly local Spanish area. Twenty minutes later we saw him striding purposefully back across the small plaza. Despite his complete lack of any Spanish, he was acknowledging everybody he passed. A typical Yorkshireman, he was throwing in comments like "*morning*", with small waves of hello, a nod of the head and a big smile as a greeting to everyone he passed. The first people he passed just blanked him completely, a couple of old ladies looked bemused. We grinned at each other, all thinking "*What is he doing?*" – "*He knows they don't speak any English*". But as he came closer, I noticed how many people did start to respond. There were smiles and nods and even a couple of waves back. They maybe didn't understand what he was saying but they did respond to how he was saying it. He was looking at people, making eye contact. His manner was genuine and sincere and his smile disarming and contagious. He didn't need words his body language and manner said everything!

One of the lines in Labi Siffre's great song *It Must be Love* is "*How can we say so much without words?*" It's a song about the love two people have for each other.

It is so true, so much of our communication is not spoken, it's inferred, through a whole host of things. Body language can convey a range of emotions, attitudes, and intentions. Our faces are capable of expressing a wide range of emotions, including happiness, sadness, anger, surprise, and fear. Searching those expressions can often provide important cues about how a person is feeling or their reaction to a situation. Hand movements, such as waving, pointing, or using thumbs up, can convey specific messages or add emphasis to verbal communication. The way we speak, including the tone, pitch, and volume of our voice, can convey meaning and emotion. It can even indicate whether a statement is a question, a command, or a joke! How we position our bodies, whether we are standing, sitting, or leaning, can communicate our level of attentiveness, interest, or dominance. Eye contact, or lack of, can give off various messages. Sustained eye contact is often associated with attentiveness, interest, or sincerity, while avoiding eye contact may indicate discomfort, shyness, or deception. Physical touch can communicate various emotions, intentions, or levels of comfort, such as a friendly handshake, an arm around the shoulder or even a hug. Standing close to someone can signal familiarity or closeness, while keeping a distance can indicate a need for personal space. These things are universal but one thing I have noted with interest is that non-verbal communication does vary across different cultures and individuals, so it's essential to consider cultural context and individual differences when deciding on your approach.

Communication is a skill that is so often underestimated. What you say and how you say it has an impact. It is the skill we need to master not only as coaches, but as human beings. It is a foundation of our relationships both on and off field. As convenient as text messaging and email is, it suffers from being two dimensional. The written word can be misinterpreted because there is no tone, body language or facial expressions to back up your words. Written communication lacks the personal touch and warmth of face-to-face or voice interactions. This can make it challenging to convey emotions effectively, build rapport, or establish a strong connection with the recipient.

I can only speak English, and as a globe-trotting coach it has thrown up some interesting situations. But as with my opening story about Ibiza shows it's not all about words.

Communication is the whole package, body language, facial expression, gestures, positioning all these tell you so much before the words come in. Watch those old silent movies from the early days of Hollywood and see wonderful examples of storytelling and communication without any words. How we listen relies heavily on these things.

One of the biggest criticisms less competent actors or even public speakers face is that they're 'wooden.' It's a term used to describe a performance that lacks naturalness, spontaneity, and emotional depth. Their delivery feels stiff and lacks authenticity. Lines are delivered in a rigid and mechanical manner, without conveying the necessary emotion. As coaches we need put our intentions across with everything we've got, if we aren't seen to believe in them why should anyone else? It reminds me of a wet and very windy night at Batley RL as a player. We were being introduced to our new coach; a wonderful man called Paul Daley, who along with Graham Murray I have so much to be grateful for. Paul was a former scrum-half whose small stature belied a big personality. After the Chairman made the general introductions, he asked Paul to say a few words. There were about 30 of us huddled together in the middle of the training field. The howling wind made it difficult to hear, I was near the back trying to pick up what he was saying. I turned at one point to the lad next to me and said *"What's he saying?"* *"I don't know"* he replied *"But whatever it is I'm in!"* I had to laugh; we couldn't really hear his plans but boy was he selling them to us. His demeanour displayed his passion and belief. It's not just what you say but how you say it! I have tried to explain Paul Daley to those that hadn't come across him. He was almost a showman; he filled a space with his presence. He could make you laugh as he did so often, but he didn't have to say much for you to know he wasn't happy. In fact, he displayed all the traits of a great communicator.

I mentioned presence earlier, all the best coaches I have met have it. When they are around you know it. The best definition I read was 'someone who projects a strong and influential aura, who commands respect and attention both physically and mentally'.

I think smiling is the most undervalued of all the communication tools. It's the top of my list. I always feel smiling puts others at ease, makes you more approachable and leaves a good first impression. A smile can help establish a connection even before any words are exchanged. Smiling also has a contagious effect. When you smile at someone, it often elicits a reciprocal smile, Whilst, it's important to smile when meeting someone for the first time, it's also essential to be genuine and authentic. There's nothing worse than a forced or insincere attempt, it's easily detected and usually has the opposite effect to the one you're aiming for.

Eye contact has lots of benefits it helps establish a connection and indicates that you are actively engaged and present in any conversation. As a coach I wanted to show respect and attentiveness toward everyone, I needed them to know that I was interested in what they had to say. We all want to feel we are acknowledged. But crucially it's not just when you are talking to individuals that eye contact is important. I have a dislike of speakers who talk above your head, I find that your message is so much more powerful when you work around the team, transferring eye contact it helps to grab and maintain their attention. It keeps them focused on your message and reduces distractions. By addressing different people in the audience with your gaze, you can create a sense of involvement and make individuals feel like active participants in the conversation.

It's important to note that cultural norms regarding eye contact can vary, and different individuals may have different preferences and comfort levels. It's essential to be mindful of cultural context, as I found in Samoa.

When I took over the team, I was introduced to what I thought at the time was a sullen group of young men who lacked interest. I can still picture the scene. I wore my biggest smile and tried to ooze enthusiasm for the task ahead. As I spoke, I tried to make eye contact with several of the players but to no avail. I asked questions and sought opinions and got zero feedback! I must admit I was nonplussed, particularly as South Sea Islanders are such a happy and gregarious people in general. Later that evening I had a meal with my new boss. I related to him how disconcerting I had found it when I spoke to the players that afternoon. He gave me a quick lesson on Samoan culture. Young people don't look older, authority figures in the eye, its seen as disrespectful. The accepted way of operating is that the person in charge gives the orders and the players carry them out without question. I am simplifying a little bit but I hadn't understood the hierarchical nature of life on the Island. As a coach I want training and preparation to be a two street. I try to encourage the players I coach to actively participate in the decision-making processes, problem-solving, and goal-setting. I want to encourage them to develop a sense of responsibility, accountability, and leadership. Most of all I need them to know that I value and respect their opinion.

It took some time to overcome this.

I talk about the importance of self-reflection elsewhere but in this particular instance I looked at everything I should've said or done. As a coach I do it naturally after every interaction whether it's a meeting, a game or a training session. I knew I had to get our communication to a place they felt comfortable with. I had a checklist I used after each training session, I would reflect and see whether I had done things the right way.

1) Did I do what I planned to do?
2) Did it change?
3) Did it develop?
4) Why?
5) Could I have done it better?
6) What worked?
7) What didn't work?
8) Did I stand in the right place?
9) Did I make any relevant points clearly?
10) Did I correct at the right time?

I would mark myself critically out of 10 on the above in an effort to get things right. But in Samoa I needed more. To prove myself worthy of their trust, to show them they were valued and could operate in positive space I needed to improve my all-round communication skills. To do this I added to my daily checklist. I was certain these extra 10 points would help me cement a coach-player relationship that could only help us be successful.

11) How did I speak to the group?
12) How did I speak to individuals?
13) Did my body language match my words?
14) Was I upbeat and enthusiastic?
15) Did I smile enough?
16) Was my eye contact long enough to show interest but not too long to be uncomfortable?
17) Did I name drop each player positively?
18) Did I engage in casual, relaxed conversation with a player or players away from the field?
19) Did I give public recognition when it was due?
20) Did I listen and crucially did I hear?

Numbers 11 and 12 were straightforward enough. I had to make sure my tone and my words matched. I had to be consistent in my messaging and I had to be authoritative without threat. I had to show I respected them as players and people. Numbers 13, 14 and 15 were really key pieces of the jigsaw. They loved their rugby and I treated them as an audience who wanted to be educated and entertained. You can't let any outside influences affect your levels of enthusiasm and your delivery. I tried to make them feel like I wanted to be there, that I cared and that, just like them, I was having the time of my life. Numbers 16 and 17 were points I had to work hard on. I mentioned above that eye contact was not a natural thing for young men dealing with authority. However, I made an effort to catch their eye, individually or as a group, whenever I could. As we got used to each other as the trust grew and they realised I would give them support and not constant condemnation, they relaxed and enjoyed being recognised for their efforts the smiles in return often came from their eyes as well as their faces. Numbers 18 and 19 were crucial. I made sure that good work was recognised and acknowledged both personally and publicly so that they understood I appreciated what they were doing and valued their efforts, but getting to know them as people without being seen to interrogate them was the vital ingredient. To instigate change and bring people with you, you have to meet them where they are. You need to know about their normal life away from rugby. Their family, their hobbies, their hopes and fears, every little piece of information on their background and dreams gives you handle on who they are and crucially how to get the best from them. It was a process over time but with these conversations and by listening to how they viewed each other, coaching them became a little easier each day. Number 20 is the foundation of good communication and one I sometimes feel is forgotten, to achieve the interaction I desire, I have to listen and listen closely. They need to see and feel that I am attentive and interested in what they say or they won't bother next time. But it's not just listening to people you have to make sure you hear them. For example, when you ask someone if they are OK and they say yes, if you are listening of course, you will hear the answer they give. But if you are really listening you will hear the tone of the answer, the emotion in their voice, the inflection put on the word. It can tell you so much than the word itself. You will know if they are really OK or not!

I had to build relationships with each player, be interested in them and their lives. I had to prove I was there to help not blame. I was non-threatening in all I did, I began with one-on-ones in informal places. On the car park, sat on a wall etc, as time went on two-way conversations became easier as trust built up. I formed a leadership group and gave them a chance to decide on issues around the team. Days off, training times, which kit to wear at training or travel. They began to enjoy the input, it wasn't their way to come and suggest things but if I put the questions in the right way, I would get some good feedback. And all the time I did everything with a big smile wherever possible. There wasn't one particular moment when I noticed what a sea change there had been in behaviour, it just gradually happened and within five months we were functioning like a team. We had open two-way conversations, they gave feedback, that sullen unresponsive group were now open and eager. That respect I mentioned for older people was still there but the messaging over several months using verbal and non-verbal communication to break down barriers was worth it. The smiles were always reciprocated and the success we had was sweeter for the togetherness we had.

I admire those people who have the ability to sum-up situations in a clear and succinct manner. I was lucky to have an opportunity to coach two particular players who had that ability. One was Martin Johnson, England's Rugby World Cup winning captain and the other was Andy Farrell, who captained both Wigan and Great Britain in Rugby League. It is no surprise that they have taken that skill into life after playing. Martin is a successful and much sought after TV pundit and Andy has forged a career as one of the World's very best coaches with Ireland and the British Lions. The clarity and conciseness I noted in their messaging are skills I have worked hard to master. Using concise language helps to convey your message clearly and without ambiguity.

It is important to remember that while being concise is important, it's also crucial to maintain the integrity and completeness of your message. Avoid oversimplifying to the point where important details or nuances are lost. Working in countries with different languages throws up the obvious problems, but it's not just the interpretation of the words that become an issue. We rely far more than we realise on intonation, on nuance, the inflections are harder to put across. It is then the way we decorate our language that takes on a key role.

Facial expressions, stance, hand movements, gestures whether we are tactile or not all become more noticeable and more relevant.

Of course, the words are at the centre of your message wherever you are. More often than not I have had to rely on an interpreter. Striking the right balance between conciseness and clarity is key when working through a translator to ensure effective and accurate communication. But I would not be being truthful if I said I had always followed my own advice. My translators have always been an 'English' speaking player and more often than not, they will translate what I say literally. I should have expected and understood this but didn't always realise.

Think about how much of a message is inferred in daily conversation, how much we expect them to read into our words. When you work through a translator that is lost. It has to be factored in; never assume they have fully understood.

My most epic fail was in Spain. In my first camp with the Spanish National team in Madrid I took the whole squad of 40 players for a defence session. I had set up tackle bags, tackle shields and cones across one half of the field. Only two of the players spoke English and one of them kindly offered to act as translator. I got everyone together and gave my words of wisdom and my instructions through my translator. We were going to start at one end of the field and work down towards the bags and cones. I was pleased with my words. I felt I had got everything across and mapped out what came next. I had tried to make eye contact with everyone but I kept looking at the translator to make sure he was repeating what I'd said. When he'd finished speaking, I looked at the group and put my thumbs up and said "OK?" (Surely the universal word and sign of agreement?). They all replied enthusiastically with thumbs up and smiles and replied "OK". I turned around and strode off to the top of the field, behind my back they jogged off to the opposite end, where the bags and shields lay. When I looked around, we were stood almost 100 metres apart! I have no idea what was said in the translation but it was obvious I hadn't been as clear and deliberate as I thought. I should have double checked my key points were understood. A mistake I vowed never to repeat as I sheepishly and apologetically jogged back to meet them!

Communication is not about speaking what we think, it's about ensuring others hear what we mean! It's not just what you say that is important but how you say it. Because as Labi Siffre said – *"We say so much without words."*

RESILIENCE

Of all the skills needed to navigate both your professional and private life, resilience is without doubt a key one.

It helps us work through challenges and setbacks. It enables us to bounce back from adversity, adapt to change, and keep moving forward. Resilience empowers us to face obstacles, maintain a positive mindset, and find solutions to problems. It allows us to persevere in the face of difficulties, build inner strength, and enhance our overall well-being. By cultivating resilience, we become better equipped to handle stress, manage emotions, and maintain healthy relationships. Ultimately, it is a vital trait that allows us to thrive in the face of life's inevitable ups and downs.

Personally, my resilience has grown over time, It's a crucial quality for a coach due to the demanding and high-pressure nature of the job. As coaches we are constantly under scrutiny, both from the public and from within our own organisations. We face criticism when results don't go as expected or when our coaching decisions are questioned. Resilience enables you to handle criticism, maintain self-belief, and stay focused on your coaching philosophy

In Samoa and Kenya particularly, dealing with unrealistic expectations created significant pressure and stress. Managing the country's expectations required maintaining a calm and composed demeanor whilst patiently outlining what a more realistic outcome may look like given the circumstances. Overall, resilience allows us to navigate the ups and downs of our journey, maintain a strong sense of purpose, and provide effective leadership to our players and staff. It helps us stay motivated, learn from setbacks, and continually strive for excellence in a highly competitive and demanding field.

The key question of course is how do we develop it? I'm not sure there's a one-size-fits-all answer but there are a combination of strategies and resources that helped me.

In my experience social support is a key factor. Building and maintaining strong relationships with family and friends provides a crucial support network during challenging times. Seek out and nurture these connections, as they can provide emotional support, practical assistance, and a sense of belonging. My wife particularly has the ability to put things into perspective. She provides insights from a different domain, just having someone give a different view more often than not can simplify an issue that may well be suffocating you. The unwavering support of my family and friends has always been a comfort, no matter how tough things are, having people who love you just for being you is an emotional anchor I need. This emotional support helps me maintain my mental wellbeing and cope with stress of high-pressure situations, demanding schedules, and the intense scrutiny we are often subjected to. I also rely on a network of trusted colleagues, mentors, and friends within sport. This group allows me to share experiences, seek advice, and gain valuable insights from others who have faced similar challenges. It is comforting to know you have people who support your coaching endeavors, who understand the sacrifices you make, and can celebrate your successes with you.

Looking after yourself with regular physical exercise offers numerous benefits from mental well-being, increasing energy levels, improving sleep quality, to keeping your weight under control, it just makes me feel better. A trick we must all learn is maintaining a good work-life balance. Coaching requires significant time and energy commitments, which can strain personal relationships and can lead to emotional and physical exhaustion, by taking time away it allows you to recharge, rejuvenate, and find equilibrium, which is vital for long-term resilience in the high-pressure coaching environment.

My resilience seems to have been tested on a regular basis. Coaching at professional level particularly is notoriously insecure. You have to be ready to face up to most things from losing your job, to moving home or moving country without much in the way of notice. Dealing with the after affects is where your mental strength comes in.

Sport has a strange way of testing you. In 2006 I was working across multiple teams as a National Academy coach for England RFU. I continued as Assistant coach for the England Sevens team but was also the Assistant Coach for the England U19s (XVs) and Head Coach of the Junior England Sevens team. It was a busy but rewarding schedule. The Senior Men's Sevens had finished as runners up on the World Series, the Junior Sevens team won silver medal at the Junior Commonwealth Games in Melbourne and the U19s finished 3rd and got a Bronze at the U19 Rugby World Cup. There were seven coaches in the National Academy who worked across all the National squads in various roles.

At the seasons close, in May, we were all summoned to an early morning meeting at Twickenham, (rugby's headquarters). I was told that my employment was being terminated. It was a complete shock. No indication was given that this was about to happen, it caught me completely by surprise. The England Senior team was in decline, it was less than three years since they had won the World Cup but results were poor. It seems a shake up was needed and a revamp of operations. I appeared to be an early casualty. I wasn't the only person but that didn't ease the feelings. I was then left with the long drive back home to Yorkshire feeling numb, feeling shocked and more than a little let down. I had no idea what lay ahead, I was fearful for the future. The timing of the decision, at the season's end, left me little opportunity to put the feelers out for a new role. Most teams would have started their recruitment already and as a relatively new convert from rugby league I didn't have an extensive network of people to fall back on for help. I rang my wife and told her the news and as you would expect she too was devastated. Within a couple of hours of arriving back home I received a call from Brian Ashton. For those of you not familiar, Brian is one of the most highly regarded coaches in the game. His reputation as a 'free thinker', who didn't conform to the accepted way, didn't always sit well with more conservative administrators but his success was admired by players, supporters and other coaches alike. Brian had been the Head of the RFU National Academy for a time and then left to take over as Head Coach at Bath RUFC, one of the games most famous club teams. I worked under him in the National Academy and enjoyed it immensely. We held many of the same views on how rugby should be played and he encouraged us all to 'coach without fear.' I was disappointed when he left but appreciated him ringing to give his commiserations – or so I thought! It was far from that. Brian began in his blunt, to the point manner. *"I can't believe it, you were one of the best coaches they had"*, I said *"Thanks Brian, I really appreciate you ringing me"*.

However, the next bit caught me completely by surprise. *"Listen there's a job assisting me at Bath as Skills and Defence coach do you want it?"* I was absolutely gob smacked, the feeling of despair at losing my job was replaced with the excited disbelief at being offered a senior post at one of the country's best teams. My wife Debs was nodding furiously, mouthing, *"Yes, yes"*. He mentioned the salary which was significantly higher than the one from the National Academy and apologised as though it might be unacceptable! Incredible I had gone from the depths of despair to uncontrolled joy in the matter of a few hours. He asked how quickly I could get down to Bath and I told him I would set off immediately. So, we jumped in the car and set off on the long drive to the West Country arriving very late, stayed with Brian and his wife Helen overnight and then went into the club the next morning. My wife, Debs, went off looking for somewhere to live whilst I met with the CEO. Bath is a beautiful and historic city and, after introductions, he insisted we went out and grab a coffee to chat. He told me how highly Brian had spoken about me and he outlined the terms of the offer. I had no hesitation in accepting. We shook hands on the deal and he said he would have the contract in the post for me to sign as soon as possible. As we shook hands his parting words were *"Welcome to Bath."*

It had been the most surreal 24 hours. In the car on our return North, we discussed the mountain of possible properties Debs had been given by local estate agents. It occurred to us that we needed to put our own house up for rent as soon as possible. We rang some letting agencies and arranged for them to view the next day. It was just before the financial crash of 2008 and house prices were rising and properties to rent in our village, in particular, didn't stay on the market too long. An agent came first thing next day and we agreed and signed. Within an hour they were back to say they had tenants and we signed to vacate the house at the end of the month. We excitedly started packing, looking at places to live and new schools in and around Bath.

If my termination by England was day one, shaking hands on the Bath job day two and renting our house out day three, then day four topped them all. We awoke to BBC news announcing that Brian Ashton had left Bath and been appointed as the new England Rugby Head Coach! I had no idea it was going to happen; Brian hadn't mentioned it. I wasn't sure of the implications for me. Brian's phone unsurprisingly was constantly busy but the CEO at Bath just ignored my calls. The promised contract through the post never arrived. I tried for days no one would answer my call. I was effectively left high and dry. I eventually had to contact a player I knew at Bath, explained the situation and asked him to get the CEO to let me know what was happening. Finally, several weeks later, I got a text to say they weren't making any appointments until the new Head Coach was in place! Because of the whirlwind of the job offer I hadn't thought about looking elsewhere for a job, now in the midst of summer when most clubs had got their recruitment on and off the pitch sorted, I was left high and dry. Just to compound my misery we had to vacate our house as we had signed a rental agreement – maybe I should have taken a leaf out of the Bath CEOs playbook and just shook hands on that!

If ever resilience was needed it was there and then. Coping with no job and no immediate prospect of getting one, having to leave our own home and find somewhere else to live. The consequences affected not just me but the whole family. Life in sport is often exciting and offers great opportunities but the insecurity it brings has to be factored in, its not for the faint hearted. I had to fall back on all the coping mechanisms I mentioned above. I relied heavily on family and friends when it looked and felt as though I had come to a dead-end on my journey. Its easy to feel worthless at these times and that the world, your world, is moving on without you but my motivation and, I suppose, strength to continue, came from a surprising source – myself!

John Neal is Professor of Practice, Sports Business Performance at Ashridge Business School. He teaches leadership, team dynamics, coaching, change and personal performance amongst many other things. He also has a lot of experience of working with elite international sports teams as a consultant psychologist. Along with all those things I regard him as a good friend. I met him when he led an Elite Coach programme at Ashridge on behalf of England Rugby. It was a fascinating look at leadership and behaviour.

A few weeks after the Bath debacle he asked if I could help him on a course for business leaders. Major international companies would send executives from all around the world for professional development at Ashridge. A part of John's delivery was a day on coaching. He needed sports people along to work with groups and add their experiences from their sporting life. It was a very enjoyable and informative day and I helped out many times over the next few years whenever I was available. I was extremely grateful to John for thinking of me and getting me involved but that wasn't the real benefit. Each time I was invited I was usually one of six or seven sports people from football, cricket and rugby. Because the participants were from all around the world, they likely had no idea who everyone was, so every session began with each one of us standing up and briefly introducing ourselves. This was a 'change moment' for me. I had to describe my journey and achievements but most of all I had to stand up and do it out loud and publicly. I had to formulate a mental highlights reel. It helped me recognise and acknowledge the experiences, relationships, and accomplishments that had shaped my journey. By recalling my past achievements and moments of success it bolstered my self-confidence and self-belief. It was a needed reminder of what I was capable of.

A mental highlights reel allows you to consciously focus on the positive aspects of your life. By recalling and reliving your best moments, achievements, and happy memories, you can shift your attention away from negative or stressful thoughts.

It is something I have used ever since. No matter how positive we are there are times when we feel low or suffer from 'imposter' syndrome. Reflecting on your mental highlights can enhance your sense of gratitude and appreciation for the good things in your life. Revisiting positive memories can uplift your mood and bring about feelings of joy and satisfaction. It serves as a mental boost, especially during challenging times.

Never lose sight of the good things and great memories in your life.

DAMIAN MCGRATH

THE MESSAGE

It was a wet, foggy, windy night at Wrexham Rugby Club. It was yet another organised trial evening for yet another launch of RGC (Rygbi Gogledd Cymru) the official regional rugby team of North Wales.

The North Wales region is almost a third of the country, yet it had no proper representation at the high table of Welsh rugby. It was merely seen as a feeder to the four powerhouse regions that dominated the game and just so happened to be all based in the south. There had been several attempts to launch RGC as the 'fifth' region all had failed due to a variety of reasons. The Southern powerhouses saw it as a waste of time and money, saw no value in establishing another team that they felt would dilute the financial and playing resources, amongst other things. I listened to the objections, no supporter base, no high level of club rugby to underpin it, no facilities, the list was long and negative. As ridiculous as it seems in such a small country, one of the objections was it was too far away!

But in 2011, I was appointed Head of Rugby in North Wales alongside Head Coach Chris Horsman and General Manager Rupert Moon. We were tasked with reigniting the North Wales dream. I had read about the previous attempts to establish the team and its failures. It wasn't just getting the players onboard with this latest venture it was getting the small local clubs dotted around the region to give up their best players once again for another shot at regional success. We did start on the front foot. The WRU were in partnership with Conwy Council who had built a new sports facility in Colwyn Bay on the north coast of Wales. We had offices, an indoor training facility, a gym that was top notch and we had an excellent multi-sports stadium, where we would play our home games. Added to that the WRU had had the foresight to establish a full-time rugby academy in partnership with Rydal School. It had recruited some talented young players from across North Wales and was being positively received.

But for all those good things it didn't answer the question of 'What's going to be different this time'? The last team they tried to establish was in partnership with the Canadian Rugby Union. The Canadians would send over their best, young, up and coming players who would join with the best in North Wales to produce a competitive team that would establish the regions reputation. What happened was that the team was mainly filled with overseas players, locals were side-lined most returned disappointed and resentful, to their clubs and no long-term development happened. When the partnership finished, and the overseas players returned home, there was nothing much left in place.

So, when we announced training for the newly launched version of RGC, uptake was understandably sparse given past experiences. Nevertheless, a trial was announced. It was made clear that the team would be made up of North Wales based players, and unlike previous versions would not play friendlies but enter the official Welsh leagues. Whilst not being included at the top level, here was a chance to establish and build a permanent, competitive team to represent the whole of North Wales. Turnout for the trial had been better than we had hoped. Over 40 players were selected.

On that wet, miserable, foggy evening in Wrexham, Chris and I looked forward with anticipation to seeing the best players available, strut their stuff. The opposition was Cobra, a local third division team who had kindly offered to give us opposition. Although we initially thought the opposition might be too weak, we were even more concerned when they only had 13 players to start the game (two more arrived later in the first half). It was a shambolic affair of mistakes and mishaps and, in the tricky conditions, chaos. As an advert for North Wales rugby, it was a disaster, it certainly didn't bode well for the launch of the team into the Welsh Leagues. The best players we could find only just edged past a local, undermanned team. It was patently obvious that the standard of rugby in North Wales was just not good enough and if progress was to be made then there would have to be changes – in organisation, in training and more importantly in approach. Not only the team but also the Academy.

It was the best thing that could have happened as far as I was concerned. That game was the springboard for player improvement and more importantly buy in from the local clubs who we relied upon for support not only in terms of players but also to help build a regional team of which everyone could be proud.

Persuading the players in the following few weeks that a new, different approach to training was needed, one that would bring positive results was much easier. Using the trial as a start point getting small wins in training led to buy in from players who began to see and feel improvements in themselves as individuals and how they operated as a team. Progress was good through the summer; a team spirit and collectiveness began to develop built on understanding and hard work and improving the little things that make a difference. Alignment across the age groups was implemented.

The next time we played was a couple of pre-season friendlies against opposition from higher leagues down south, it was a far cry from that foggy night in Wrexham. The players who took the field were fast, skillful and very much a team. They won convincingly scoring some spectacular tries. The changes we made were easier to do using our first trial game as a starting point. Without that fiasco it may have been a more difficult proposition.

But how could that influence our relationship with the local clubs whose support was vital going forward? Well, we couldn't tell them that their players were poor and the standard of rugby locally was inadequate. That approach would get us nowhere. No one likes to have their shortcomings pointed out. It would only cause tension if we were seen to come in and laud our improvements and demand a rise in standards to help us. Fortunately, the foggy night in Wrexham helped us immeasurably. The players often harked back to that night and laughed at what happened, I decided to use that humour to highlight positive change and get across the message we needed to make. Our analyst, Andy Jones, put together a short video.

The first part was from the trial, made up of clips of the mishaps and numerous errors, (ball hitting players in the face, players dropping the ball, players tripping over each other, players comically turning their backs and not watching what's going on as the ball went past them, a calamity of errors). These were shown with circus music to give the impression of chaotic clowns who didn't know what was happening. It segued into number of clips of the same players several months later executing skills and scoring spectacular tries with upbeat rock music. The message was look what we can do, look at how change has occurred for the better, the standards we are bringing in will only help all local clubs and players.

We showed it for the first time at the North Wales Rugby Committee meeting. Full of club representatives who were by nature resistant to change and particularly hostile to anything that might affect their clubs. It was a game changer they loved it laughed at the start and applauded the improvements. Now they could see the regional team may well be a positive, their endorsement whilst not effusive was certainly much more positive than we could ever have hoped. The bandwagon was rolling.

How you put your message across can have significant effect on how it's received. Pointing out the obvious is not always well received, particularly when it questions abilities or outlook. By presenting facts in a different way the outcome can be significantly different. In this instance I didn't overtly tell the local clubs that they weren't good enough I simply showed something that wasn't threatening but uplifting.

AUTHENTICITY
BEING YOU OR BEING A PERFORMER

Being authentic is a key pillar to being a successful leader. It's another one of those hot topics which along with culture you can read thousands of books and articles on. Being true to your own personality, values, and spirit.

The real me, the authentic me is an insecure, introverted, shy individual who feels awkward in company and hates small talk with a passion. I love sitting and listening to others tell stories and jokes without the pressure of doing the same. I feel comfortable in the crowd not as a stand-alone, or front and centre. It seems laughable now, but I remember at school thinking obscurely that I could never become a Member of Parliament because you had to stand up and make your maiden speech in front of a watching world, that very thought filled me with dread. I have never really shrugged that version of me off, its still there. What I did have was a need to make a mark, I had a feeling I could succeed, I couldn't just sit still and be comfortable, but I always felt someone would see I had things to offer.

However, it took me many years to realise I could never aspire to be the coach and leader I wished to be by taking that approach. Was I going to continue as the insecure, unassured historical me or choose to learn and act my way into becoming something I felt I could be and needed to be? But then would I truly be authentic? There are behaviourists who see authenticity not as a trait – something you either have or you don't have – but as the outcome of a process of becoming your own person, the lifelong process of learning about yourself. It derives from the Greek word *"authenteos"* which essentially became to mean self-authoring.

My self-belief may have been well hidden but I have always felt that I am good at what I do. My coaching at whatever level has always been well received. I was sure that this was more than enough to get me where I wanted to be, that my work would speak for itself. I was a part of lots of successful coaching teams on the national and international stage, but I was always one of the supporting cast. I may have been well thought of by my peers but the decision makers on the big roles had no idea who I was or more importantly what I could really do. I felt awkward and incapable of pushing myself forward, I always felt my talents and what I could bring to the table should and would be enough. In my mind I insisted that my work would speak for itself. Yet I watched as people who I didn't feel were any better or more talented than me were promoted or got the plum jobs simply, it seemed to me, because they sold themselves in a much more effective way.

Now I really felt I was being authentic, I felt the quality of my work, my results, experience and my work ethic should be more than enough, but clearly this wasn't the case. I wasn't comfortable or confident enough to step outside my comfort zone, but I realised that if I wanted to move forward, I had to put my 'head above the parapet', take the risk of 'blowing my own trumpet' whatever idiom you might wish to use.

I was a classic example of what Herminia Ibarra calls the "*authenticity paradox*." It's when you find yourself facing a choice between being yourself or doing what it takes to be effective. You want to move up or be successful and have more impact, but you have mixed feelings about the transition and are more than a little unsure. You feel you will have to sacrifice your values and your integrity, and you don't want to become like all those people who were way less sincere or much more political. Do you sacrifice substance for style? If I stick to my approach because I feel morally justified in being authentic, am I being too cautious? Professor Ibharra points out my conundrum quite clearly;

"You find yourself facing a choice between being yourself or doing what it takes to be effective. What do you do? What works? You will not change without making a conscious effort. You have to take on a persona that allows you to get where you want to be and achieve what you feel you can."

Professor Ibharra looks at some of the ways in which we define authenticity to see if they can help us sort out some of these questions.

"The most common way we define authenticity is being true to yourself. But that raises the question: True to which self? Your old self, today's self, or your future self? And if it's your old self or today's self, does that mean being authentic condemns you to being as you've always been? Of course not. Often, we'll be true to a self that we want to become or an aspirational self – that's what we talk about when we say "fake it till you make it".

A second way that we define authenticity is being sincere – in other words, saying what you mean and meaning what you say. As it turns out, the word "sincere" has a really interesting origin. It comes from two Latin roots "sine," without, and "cera," wax, that together mean "without wax."

That phrase comes from ancient Rome where it was a common practice for statue merchants to hide any flaws in their statues with wax. The more scrupulous merchants and the ones who didn't want to be dishonest would hang a sign outside their shops that said "Sine Cera."

To be sincere you have to be able to communicate it, but we all know the first principle of effective communication is tailoring it to your audience."

Sometimes the quality you bring or the values you have aren't always as clear as you might think. It is imperative that your message is delivered in a clear and memorable manner.

A third definition of authenticity is being true to your values. Sometimes using compelling language in your arguments or in explaining your stance can be difficult when the facts you feel speak for themselves but embellishing your point of view or approach rather than relying on legitimate logical analysis is sometimes needed even if you value substance over style. I still think I'm authentic, I still rely heavily on knowing my subject and still believe in letting the facts stand out, however what has changed is my delivery. I found I could create a learning environment that encouraged people, that engaged people and more importantly valued people. It didn't just happen but the confidence in knowing your stuff and belief in your vision and how to get there has allowed me to stand up in meetings and conferences and get my message across. Coaching and leading people of all abilities, from children to international stars is still daunting but my "new" authentic self (the person I have become) allows me to accomplish what I want to accomplish – what I always felt I could accomplish.

Every time I speak publicly, every training session I do I treat as a performance. I prepare, I mentally rehearse and I try and deliver with the right amount of communication, content and timing. And that's the key as a coach, you must always be at your best no matter how you are feeling or who your audience is. It is not you pretending to be someone you aren't, it is you striving to always be the best you can be and making sure everyone sees that's who you are. Why try and be fake when being real takes less effort!

RECOGNITION OR APPRECIATION?

It is the ultimate gift.
It costs nothing but is worth everything.
We all crave it.
The best people give it.
To be recognised for your efforts and valued for who you are!

When people receive recognition and appreciation for their hard work it can have a number of effects, all of them positive. It boosts their motivation. By recognising their efforts, you are acknowledging their contributions and showing them that their work is valued, which in turn encourages them to continue giving their best. Being recognised and appreciated fosters a positive work environment and boosts team morale. It creates a sense of fulfillment and job satisfaction among team members, leading to increased happiness and engagement in their work. People are more likely to feel connected to the team and the organisation as a whole.

This sense of loyalty increases their commitment and reduces the chances of turnover. People are more likely to stay in a positive work environment where their efforts are acknowledged and appreciated. When individuals feel valued and recognised for their contributions, they are more inclined to work with others and share their knowledge and skills. This creates a supportive and cooperative team dynamic.

When your team and staff feel appreciated, they are more likely to think outside the box, take risks, and contribute new ideas. By acknowledging and valuing these innovative contributions, you can foster a culture of continuous improvement and creativity. When team members receive positive feedback and recognition for their achievements, they gain confidence and are motivated to further develop their skills. This can lead to higher performance levels and career advancement opportunities.

We often use these words interchangeably and think of them as the same thing. But while they're both important there's a big difference between them. Recognition is about what people do; Appreciation is about who they are. Recognition is appropriate and necessary when it's earned and deserved. Appreciation, however, is important all the time. I don't think I've ever met anyone who didn't want to be appreciated. We all want some kind of validation, to know that what we do or who we are is well thought of. Never underestimate the impact of saying thank you and meaning it. I say it and mean it every day whether its someone opening a door, serving in a shop or just attending a meeting. It's good manners but it lets people know you appreciate what they do.

At training sessions, I will always make an effort to interact with each player as they warm-up or as they prepare for training, putting my arm around their shoulder, shaking their hand, sharing a joke or just asking how they are. It is my way of connecting with them and I will strive to praise them by name in some small way as we progress – it allows me to publicly show them that I recognise their efforts.

After a tour or even as I leave a role, I will drop each player and staff member a private message to convey my appreciation of their efforts and let them know I valued everything they did. In the modern world WhatsApp makes that much easier to do, but in times past I would even hand post them a brief written note along the same lines. But there are much simpler ways to do it on a regular basis. Put down your phone, turn away from your computer, and genuinely listen to people. Check in with the people you work with. Ask how they're doing, let them know you genuinely care. *"People don't care how much you know until they know how much you care."*

Tell people what you value about them. Doing this proactively – not because someone did something great or because you want something from them. It can positively affect how your players and staff feel about themselves, your relationship with them, and the culture of the team. Creating a culture of appreciation is important as it creates loyalty, trust and builds connection within the team. Everyone likes to feel appreciated and recognised for what they do. At work, at home and in every aspect of life, being recognised and appreciated for the contribution you make can foster a level of loyalty, gratitude and happiness that becomes the foundation of everything you do. I would not be able to operate and work without my wife's unwavering support and advice. I never miss an opportunity to show her how grateful I am.

For coaches the importance of recognising your players or staff for the results they achieve or their contribution to the team is paramount in ensuring they feel happy, rewarded and maintain high standards. When you prioritise recognition in the way you operate, it can have a positive, powerful impact on your overall performance.

I can only speak from personal experience but as a young, eager assistant at Leeds Rhinos I was lucky enough to meet and work for a man who embodied everything a great leader should be. I have written earlier about Graham Murray, the Australian coach who completely transformed my coaching. Up until I met him I had never really given much thought to the psychological side of coaching, I understood being good with people was important but I had focused almost exclusively on the tactical and technical side of the game. There isn't space to document everything he did. There were so many small things which made a lasting difference, but one in particular had a huge impact on me.

One Friday evening we were the televised Sky TV game. We had travelled south to play the London Broncos who had just been taken over by the entrepreneur, Richard Branson. They were riding high in the league and boasted some big overseas names on their team list. It was one of those key games that might shape the final table. We were losing and struggling with 20 minutes to go, but our substitutions made a huge difference, and we came back to win in good style. In the after-match TV interview, Graham was congratulated on the great win but also lauded for his substitutions, which the commentary team and pundits felt swung the match. Without hesitation he said, *"That wasn't me. My assistant Damian McGrath made the call. He changed the formation and brought the right players on in the right place. He deserves the praise"*.

How often do you come across a high profile leader pushing the plaudits onto someone else, especially in such a public manner? Most see it as a sign of weakness. Not Graham he wanted everyone to see that success was built on everyone's contribution. If anything, it made him even more popular and respected. For me it was a big moment on live TV. I didn't know that Muzza was going to do it and as you can imagine it only increased my admiration of the man. It lifted my profile, boosted my confidence, but most of all it showed how much I was valued and trusted. My self-belief skyrocketed. The public recognition was the catalyst my career needed but the boost to my self-esteem was immeasurable. But what was interesting was the effect it had on the rest of the staff. We were all in the dressing room watching the interview as we celebrated with the players. They knew that we had a man in charge who would appreciate our efforts and would make sure people knew about them.

Recognition is about giving positive feedback based on results or performance – everyone wants their good work to be applauded. Appreciation, is about acknowledging a person's inherent value. The point isn't their accomplishments. It's their worth as a colleague and a human being. This distinction matters because recognition and appreciation are given for different reasons. Even when people succeed, inevitably there will be failures and challenges along the way; If you focus solely on praising positive outcomes, on recognition, you miss out on lots of opportunities to connect with and support your team members – to appreciate them.

CULTURAL INTELLIGENCE
WE DON'T SEE THINGS AS THEY ARE, WE SEE THEM AS WE ARE!

Cultural Intelligence is a relatively new phrase, certainly one I hadn't encountered until recently but it certainly describes a skill I have had to try and perfect over the course of my career

It refers to your ability to function effectively in diverse cultural contexts. To be culturally intelligent you must have the knowledge, skills, and attitudes required to understand, adapt to, and interact with people from different cultural backgrounds. It goes beyond simply being aware of other cultures; it encompasses the ability to navigate and engage with cultural differences in a respectful and productive manner. To have Cultural Intelligence you need cultural knowledge: This includes an understanding of the cultural values, beliefs, traditions, communication styles and practices of different groups.

You may feel that it's only common sense but despite my long experience of working overseas it still catches me out from time to time. On my first day in Kenya I sat in on a disciplinary meeting for one of our senior players. He had missed several training sessions in the previous two weeks and, indeed, was late for the meeting we were sat in. When questioned about his recent behaviour and the reasons behind it he said it was because of the influence of a local Witch Doctor! Now that wasn't the answer I was expecting. I almost laughed out loud thinking how preposterous that was but I was the only one smiling. It still happens in parts of Africa, there are 52 tribes in Kenya each with its own way of operating and belief system. It was a quick reminder of making sure you understand people's lives before you judge them.

To being culturally intelligent, you have to have cultural AWARENESS, being conscious and sensitive to cultural differences and recognising the impact they can have on interactions and relationships. It involves recognising and challenging our own biases and assumptions about other cultures.

This was never more apparent than in Samoa. The South Sea islands have very strong traditions which can seem very much at odds with our western views. Samoan culture is of Polynesian heritage and is proudly based on fa'a Samoa which translates as 'The Samoan Way'. Many Samoans live in tight-knit villages where family and the idea of 'tribe' is everything. Fa'a Samoa is holistic, meaning that it is understood as encompassing all facets of the Samoan way of life. For many, adhering to fa'a Samoa is closely associated with honouring one's family.

Stories of genealogies and legends are passed down and elaborated through the generations. Village storytellers are highly respected and honoured. Samoan society is based on a system known as 'fa'a Matai'. In this system, society is organised by extended families (aiga), with each family having its own 'Matai' (chief), titles that are connected to certain districts, villages, and plots of family land. Individuals in the aiga are expected to be generous with their possessions and prioritise the interests of the group or community over their own. For example, people tend to be communal and share their goods rather than prizing individual ownership. Matai are responsible for administrative duties and maintaining the traditions and customs of the village. Matai are also seen as spiritual caretakers of all those who fall under their authority. The status of Matai is highly respected among the community and wields a great deal of power.

During my stay a couple of the national team players had a falling out with the Chief of their villages and were banished, meaning they had to leave home and move into the capital, Apia, away from family and friends for a lengthy period of time. Understanding the hierarchical system was key to understanding life on that beautiful island. Age automatically gave you respect. Whereas we operate in a system where respect has to be earned, there it is given by right to your elders. I saw this in play at the Samoan Rugby Union, some of the employees were either out of their depth or just downright lazy. Consultants from New Zealand, appointed by World Rugby, came to improve governance and assess the way the union was run. When talking privately I knew that many of the younger people there were very critical of the 'dead wood' that were employed by the SRU. But I found out that in meetings none of them would criticise those same individuals that privately they had no time for. It turned out they were Matai's and wielded much power in their villages but also, they were elders and no one would ever publicly disrespect an elder – it wasn't the Samoan way.

Being adaptable, being able to adjust your behaviour, communication style and attitude to fit in is vital. It includes being flexible and open-minded when encountering new cultural situations and being able to modify your approach accordingly. In Kenya corruption is a part of daily life at all levels. It is unavoidable to get things done you have to factor that in. To get the pitches marked you need to slip the groundsman a few coins – even though that's what he's paid to do but when he does it and how efficiently often depends on the cash changing hands. Even getting your passport stamped in an acceptable time at the immigration office requires the passing of money under the table. My first encounter with this unavoidable practice was when I selected two players for the Commonwealth Games Squad who were trainee police officers. I was told it was part of a government initiative and that as international sportsmen they were allowed to be released for training camps and international competition.

They simply had to be signed off by their commanding officer. Simply! That is certainly an understatement. My Team Manager and I made an appointment with him to get the required forms signed off. We were invited into his office where we explained why we were there. "*Yes*" he said he was the man who needed to sign off on the players but how quickly he signed off of course depended on us. I looked blankly at him then the Team Manager. I had no idea what he meant but my colleague certainly did. After a bit of haggling, we agreed to buy him two cows in return for him signing the release forms there and then. Welcome to Kenya!

I'm often asked about the differences in the countries or sports in which I worked, it's difficult to sometimes give a definitive answer. If you were blindfolded and taken to Germany or Canada and then the blindfold was taken off, the first thing you would see were people who looked just like you, it could be England. The shops are more or less the same, the clothes, buildings, cars etc. It is only when you enter into the minutiae of daily life the differences become apparent. Their approach to driving, parking, queuing, pedestrians, bureaucracy, food, drink, acceptable behaviour, humour, expectations, so many things that make you realise it's not what you are used to. In Kenya or Samoa in the South Pacific it is much more obvious but wherever you are the first hurdle to deal with is perspective and perception. Yours and theirs. Their view of the world and point of view has to be considered. Their beliefs, biases, judgements, experiences, preferences are who they are, to understand how to connect with them you need to have an idea of how they look at things and more importantly why. In order to shift a persons' perspective on an issue it's important to understand why they feel the way they do. What are the perceptions and beliefs that are giving them a particular perspective? Once those perceptions are clear you can begin to change their perspective. But a word of caution as I found out, people hold onto their beliefs and perceptions tightly so care must be taken in how you approach it.

When I meet a team or a player for the first time it's impossible to know them. You may know of them, but nothing more than that. I need to find out their view of the world, their ambitions, their interests and their background. Without this knowledge how could I possibly know if I am pressing the right buttons or if the plan, I am outlining for the team corresponds to their own plan of the future!

SELF REFLECTION

I have practiced self-reflection all my life, initially without realising it and then, as I began to realise its benefits, intentionally. Self-reflection is considered a natural human trait. It is the ability to examine your own thoughts, your emotions and your actions.

Like a lot of people, I wanted to be liked, I was young, insecure and shy. I might not be the coolest kid in class but I didn't want to be seen negatively. I would often have the answers when the teacher asked a question, but I didn't want to share in case I was wrong and people laughed. I was good at remembering jokes but didn't tell them incase they weren't regarded as funny. I tried to stay anonymous, a background artiste. But every day I would think about the situations I had been in and berate myself privately that I had missed opportunities to show my knowledge or capabilities. It was self-reflection but not the best type. I engaged in excessive self-criticism, focussing too much on my flaws, mistakes and shortcomings, it resulted in negative self-judgment. Self-reflection has the potential to become unproductive and by dwelling on negative thoughts and emotions I began to overthink and became indecisive and hesitant, fearing potential mistakes or negative outcomes. It was important that I learned these lessons because whilst self-reflection is such a key part of a coach's toolbox it has to be used properly. Self-reflection does involve accepting and acknowledging your mistakes or honestly assessing your actions, behaviors, and decisions but it should help you take responsibility for your actions and learn from them. Accepting your wrong is a crucial part of self-reflection because it allows you to make amends or take corrective actions as necessary. It is an opportunity for growth and self-forgiveness.

Self-reflection can occur in various forms, such as contemplating past experiences, as I am doing by writing this book or by evaluating your behavior on a daily basis or by questioning your beliefs when times get tough. It is a fundamental aspect of human cognition and plays a crucial role in emotional intelligence, self-awareness, and decision-making.

While self-reflection is a natural inclination, the extent to which people engage in it can vary. Some people may naturally engage in more self-reflection, while others may need to consciously cultivate this practice. As a young coach I used journaling, a knock-on of my teaching days when writing lesson plans was part of daily life. I soon got into the habit of outlining my session in its simplest form and then writing it out in full afterwards. I did this because I always find training sessions develop around a broad theme and can deviate depending on circumstances. I would write the session out and then make notes around things I needed to be aware of next time. A change to a drill or practice, what worked or didn't work, if what I did was relevant or if I needed more or less space to work on particular topics. I found it very useful but more so when I began to add more subjective things. Was I stood in the right place? Could everyone see and hear me? Did I explain clearly? Was I loud enough? Did I speak too much? Did I correct too much? Did I ask questions? Did I ask the right questions?

I used any training footage I could get to help with my delivery. I always saw similarities to stage performers. They know that whether it's an afternoon matinee or the main Saturday night show they must always give the audience the best performance they can. Every day on the training field I felt compelled to do the same. Energy, enthusiasm, passion and knowledge had to be there if it wasn't I had to reflect on what was missing and why.

Putting down my thoughts for this book has required a great deal of self-reflection. I can see the countless times I made mistakes, and how often I repeated them because I refused to accept I was wrong. But I can see, as I grew personally and matured as a coach, how I was prepared to be more vulnerable. I began to own my mistakes; I would let people know what I didn't know rather than pretending I had all the answers. I would think hard about my approach and, if things weren't going well, be prepared to change course rather than stubbornly soldiering on. I listened to advice and stopped dismissing things the earlier version of me wouldn't have countenanced. It is no good having experiences if you aren't prepared to learn from them. Knowing when it's time to step away can be a challenging decision.

If I needed a reminder about listening to advice, about heeding warnings and being prepared to walk away if things aren't right, then the last 12 months have brought that home to me in no uncertain terms. After leaving my role with German National team I was looking forward to finally spending some time at home. But within a week of being back I had a call, out of the blue, from the Kenyan Rugby Union. Things weren't going well for them, they wanted make a change and had heard I was available. For those not aware, Kenya Rugby Sevens had been one of the top Rugby Sevens teams in the world for the previous eight or nine years. They had a reputation, power and speed but I knew from coaching against them that their achilles heel was their poor level of skill and general hand eye co-ordination.

On reflection I had two emotions, firstly, I was delighted that they had reached out to me because I was the type of experienced coach they needed. Secondly, I was excited because I genuinely thought that here was a place where I could make a difference especially given that improving basic skills was my thing. The first warnings came from two very trusted sources. One was a former coach who had left several years earlier as he couldn't work in the environment. He was now doing great things elsewhere. The other was a former international administrator, who had a very good handle on the country and their rugby board through his extensive business dealings. They were both unequivocal in their message *"Don't do it!!"* They told me of the corruption, the double dealing, the cronyism, the nepotism, the trust issues and the financial problems. I should have listened; I had worked in many different environments and I really thought I could handle everything and anything. It couldn't be worse than anywhere else I'd been!!! Famous last words.

Kenya's Rugby was in disarray. The sevens team had scraped qualification to the Sevens World Cup by the skin of its teeth and was staring at the very real likelihood of relegation from the World Series. The Union had crippling financial issues that no one had mentioned to me, and the current board of directors were putting all their attention and whatever resources (including the sevens budget) they still had, into trying to qualify for the 15s World Cup in France. I should have had an inkling of the situation; the offices were some old shipping containers and they had no kit to give me! The country had had its one and only success on the World Series in 2016 (six years earlier). That team was built around a 'golden generation' of players who had come to the fore at the same time. The rugby mad followers in the country now expected success as a given. But now those players had retired and there was a talent gap. There had been no development, no talent ID, no coach development. There were lots of athletic players but the standard in comparison to the rest of the rugby world was miles away. However, that sense of entitlement in the rugby community remained. But I was confident, as I always am, that I could make a difference and improve the players I had at my disposal.

We began with preparations for the 2022 Commonwealth Games, a six-week residential camp funded by the National Olympic Committee. The Games were generally a success. We bowed out in the Quarter-finals to the World Champions, New Zealand after a good tussle. We took that upturn into the final leg of 2022 World Series in Los Angeles finishing in sixth place. The players and staff were receptive to the new ideas I introduced and worked hard. I could see a way forward. Then all the warnings I had ignored began to bite.

Where to start? We weren't paid for four months (Staff and players); acceptable facilities were nonexistent. No food at training, no insurance, we couldn't afford fuel to transport players to training venues, the list went on and on. Our preparation phase for the next season was rendered nonexistent. My friends advised walking away, colleagues whose advice I trusted said likewise. They basically told me I was on a hiding to nothing, why tarnish your reputation in a role in which you cannot succeed? I knew they were right but I still thought I could change things, was that blind optimism or just pride? I thought long and hard but on reflection I was blind to the fact that these issues we faced weren't new. It was a failing programme and had been long before I arrived.

We were in a no-win situation almost from the beginning. It was impossible to make the changes and install the processes that would allow us to build on our early successes. As an outsider stepping into Kenya Rugby, I was shocked at what I found. How can anyone expect a high-performance team to operate when it has nothing around it that can be described as such. In comparison to all our rival competitors we were light years behind. There was no system, no plan, no coordinated development pathway, no support structure to help staff or players and most importantly no coach education fit for purpose. As you might expect the season was an unmitigated disaster, but I ignored all my own advice. The consequences were obvious. Job satisfaction disappeared, stress and anxiety crept in. Frustration and feelings of powerlessness began to erode my self-confidence and self-esteem. No matter what we did we couldn't effect the changes needed. Too late I realised I needed to get out.

Engaging in self-reflection should allow for greater self-awareness and better decision-making, I wouldn't accept that stepping away didn't necessarily equate to failure. It's important to regularly evaluate your goals, values, and well-being to determine when the "try, try again" approach may no longer be applicable and when it's appropriate to make a change

My inability to heed the self-reflection that had served me so well, to ignore advice from friends and colleagues whose opinions I have always trusted has been a harsh lesson, one I didn't think I would have so late in my career. Regular introspection is vital and your experiences should allow you to make informed decisions on the situation you face. I led the team so must bear the consequences of the outcome but it wasn't so much the failure of the team that hurt me it was my own failure to act appropriately when the messages were clear and obvious.

Naturally I did much soul searching (self-reflection) in the aftermath, I had to admit my shortcomings to myself and those friends, mentors and colleagues whose opinions I set great store by. This was the most positive thing I could have done. Their perspective helped me change mine. Reframing is a powerful tool in dealing with failure. By reframing, you can shift your view and find a different interpretation of the situation. It allows you to accept failure and learn from it. You acknowledge that sometimes certain failures are beyond your control. Accepting this can help alleviate feelings of self-blame or guilt. I was encouraged to focus on the lessons I could take from the experience and acknowledge that failures happen to everyone. Everyday is an education no matter how old or how experienced you are.

CONFUSING DEFEAT WITH FAILURE

In a risky game of individual winners, losing is ever present.

When legendary 20-time champion jockey AP McCoy retired in 2015, he was hailed for a record-breaking career. *"I rode 4,357 winners, but I rode 14,000 losers too,"* he remarked. His winning percentage of about 25% may have been among the best, but he lost most of the time.

"If everything you do in your preparation – studying the form, diet – is geared up for the best chance of winning, what happens when you lose?" he says. *"People need to be better equipped for dealing with defeat. It's a losing sport. You spend the majority of your career losing. It's very tough mentally and riders are often the first people to blame. You are under constant pressure to get it right. One of the most valuable things I learned is emotional intelligence. Controlling what I can control and understanding that losing isn't going to define my work."*

Not everyone can win, so as a coach you can't define yourself just by your win percentage. There are so many factors that come into play. That old saying "you can only play the cards you're dealt" is one I've heard many times meaning that you have to work with the circumstances or resources you have available, rather than dwelling on what you don't have. The expression emphasises the importance of making the best out of the situation at hand. Life often presents us with various challenges and circumstances that are beyond our control. While we may not have control over the initial hand we are dealt, we do have control over how we play those cards and navigate through. Instead of fixating on what we lack or what could have been, it's more productive to focus on leveraging our strengths, making the most of the opportunities available, and adapting our strategies as needed. It encourages us to be resourceful, resilient, and creative in finding solutions and achieving our goals. By accepting the hand we've been dealt and playing it to the best of our abilities, we can find ways to succeed, grow, and overcome obstacles. It's about embracing the present moment, being adaptable, and making the most of the circumstances we find ourselves in but even then, we can find ourselves in a no-win situation. How do you decide if you have failed or if you've just been defeated?

First of all, you have to decide what you regard as a win, a failure or just a defeat. My experiences in Kenya were the toughest I'd ever encountered as a coach, for the first time in my career I felt I couldn't make a difference, there were many times I felt totally helpless and unsure of what to do next. At the end of an exhausting, miserable and draining season we were relegated from the World Series. As you can imagine the keyboard warriors piled on social media to point the finger of blame. I hadn't just lost I had totally failed. I had never been in this position before. What I needed was someone to put it in perspective and fortunately I had some good people to help me do that. In their eyes I had simply been defeated by circumstances. They pointed out how much I couldn't control and what I'd achieved despite the events that overtook us. My wife even printed out the messages of thanks from players for helping them improve! I gave everything I could but circumstances certainly beat me. I felt at times that the programme didn't need a coach but a magician. No facilities, going unpaid for four months, the list seemed endless, but by reframing the experience the despair I first felt, has ebbed away and that my experience in Kenya won't, as AP McCoy said, define my work!

FROM THEN TO NOW

Isn't it amazing what you keep?

One of the down sides of working overseas is having to put your things, your life, into storage. A couple of years ago I needed some documents for an insurance issue. I wasn't sure where they were but I entered a storage bay and began hunting through boxes. I eventually found them but I also came across some old lesson plans from my teaching days. No idea why I'd hung onto them but I wasted an hour or so reading through them, much to my wife's annoyance! One of them caught my attention it was an English lesson. According to the notes it was to get the children to see themselves in ten years' time, either through an article in a magazine, newspaper headlines, a TV report or in a poem. We were trying to get them to look at what they wanted to be and what type of person they'd liked to be thought of. As an example, I gave them my poem. I think it's clear I am no William Wordsworth but I had a shot. Apart from the fact I remember desperately trying to find words that rhymed, (I was impressed with my use of spurious), it was at a time in my life where I realised teaching wasn't enough and although I wasn't sure what it was, I really wanted, I knew I was ready for a leap of faith, and change direction. There was a big world out there!

If you had to do the same, how would you see yourself ten years down the line? Would you change for the better or for the worse?

TEN YEARS' TIME

If I was walking down the street, am I a man I'd like to meet?

Will I be smart or will I be clever, a positive man who never
says never?

Or will I be careworn, sad and regretful,

Forever risk averse, constantly neglectful?

I do hope if I happen to bump into me,

I recognise the leader I want people to see.

Fulfilled, still eager and never spurious,

deeply passionate and eternally curious.

The traits that drive me forward, even now, eagerness, passion and curiosity were obviously at the forefront of my mind, I wanted to be a leader, I wanted to be challenged. So fast forward to now, many, many years down the track. I thought about those hopes. How would the younger me view me now? Would he recognise the man I hope I've become?

NOW

As I was walking down the hill I saw him there upon the sill,

A smiling man, happy and tall whose face and look I should recall.

Was he a mate, a friend from the past, a passing connection that didn't last?

No, he was me, that man in the pane whose reflection I caught as I went down the lane.

Still eager, still keen, still looking to learn, but with an unmistakeable passion that continues to burn.

Despite all my faults, mistakes and errors I think the younger me would appreciate the fruits of my endeavours

What I'm trying to say, what I really mean, is that I think I have become the man I always should have been.

On reflection I was setting myself some early goals and even predicting how I might be if I didn't achieve them. I would never have guessed back then as I searched for the next step that I would embark on a roller coaster ride around the world and that the same passion to learn and move forward is still as strong as ever!

DAMIAN MCGRATH

PAVEMENTS AND GRASS VERGES
IT STARTS WITH ME AND ENDS WITH WE!

Although I was predominantly a PE teacher, life in a Middle School necessitated teaching a variety of other subjects as part of my weekly timetable.

One such was Social Studies, a mixture of history, geography and sociology. One of the topics we covered was social standing – looking at the class divide – how people lived, worked and played in their particular areas. I put on a video for the class that took them into the poorer areas of a major city and contrasted it with the view from the more affluent parts of town.

In our staff planning lessons we had outlined what we were looking for from the children when we began to discuss the film. We were trying to get the children to recognise the causes of poverty and how it manifests itself in the way we live. This was a group of children living in inner city Leeds, some were living in the conditions seen in parts of the film.

At the end I asked them for the first thing that came to mind. I got the usual answers, *"the nice area has bigger houses and nice cars"*, *"the poorer area has more takeaway shops and appears cramped and run down."* But one girl put her hand up and said *"Pavements and grass verges."* This caught me by surprise as it wasn't an answer I was expecting and I must admit I dismissed it almost immediately. *"Good try but I'm not sure that's what we are after."*

But the girl next to her agreed. Intrigued I had to ask why. *"Well in all the shots of the nice area"* she said *"The streets were clean and well-*

kept; the grass verges were tidy and there was no litter on the pavements but in the poorer parts of town they were dirty and full of rubbish. The gardens were scruffy and people parked wherever they wanted." This started a discussion I hadn't bargained on but was so well thought out. The children came to the conclusion that an area wasn't necessarily defined by its money or its resources but by its people. How they thought and how they lived. The standards they accepted.

Simply put they thought people in nice places were proud of what they had and worked together to keep it that way. They accepted the rules and stuck to them (parking was one they highlighted), they self-policed in terms of litter and what was and what wasn't acceptable. It made it a safer environment for everyone. Yes, they agreed money and resources were important but ultimately people make the choice to drop litter, park on double yellow lines or on pavements. Their big take away was that they felt the people living in the affluent area cared about how they lived and where they lived whereas the opposite was often the case in poorer areas. People tended to look out for themselves and crucially from their own experiences it only took a minority to pull everyone else down. Now I know that there is far more to it than that but I couldn't really find fault with their viewpoint.

The children's view was based on what places looked like and backed up my Grandad's line about dressing to impress. *"There's only one thing worse than being poor, that's looking poor!"* While the appearance of a place is not the sole indicator of its operation, it can play a crucial role in shaping the atmosphere and effectiveness of the space. A thoughtful and well-designed environment can support the desired behaviors, interactions, and outcomes sought by a team.

In sporting terms, culture refers to the shared values, beliefs, attitudes, behaviors, and norms that exist within a team. It encompasses the collective mindset, traditions, and practices that influence the team's identity and performance. Sporting culture shapes the way athletes, coaches, and staff members approach their roles, collaborate with one another, and engage with fans and sponsors.

A strong sporting culture establishes a set of principles and expectations that guide the behavior and decision-making of individuals within the team. It influences how team members communicate, handle adversity, work together, and strive for success. A positive and healthy sporting culture promotes attributes such as teamwork, respect, discipline, accountability, sportsmanship, and continuous improvement. It sets the tone.

So, we know what it is, but where does it start? What does it rely on? It certainly isn't a 'one man band.' Culture is a collective phenomenon it needs everyone to buy in, to care. But in my experience, it relies, particularly in the beginning, on one person – the Coach. They have the power to design, shape and align a team culture that matters. A good coach generates this commitment to a cause that's founded on their compelling and inspiring vision that players and staff alike can identify with.

The coach brings their beliefs, values, behaviors, and practices to a group. By articulating and promoting these guiding principles, they shape the culture by defining what is important and what behaviors are encouraged or discouraged. They serve as role models for their players and staff, as their words, actions and behaviours are observed and imitated by others reinforcing the cultural values and expectations.

When a leader establishes a good culture, they rely on the support and active participation of their workforce to maintain and sustain that culture ultimately, a good culture is a collective effort that requires the engagement and support of the entire team. When players and staff actively participate in upholding the cultural values, it strengthens the culture and reinforces the coach's efforts to establish a positive and productive work environment.

I mention elsewhere the admiration I had for Graham Murray, with whom I worked at Leeds Rhinos where I was his Assistant Coach. Until our paths crossed, I had never given culture too much thought. Yet here was a man who brought his beliefs, values and practices to a large sporting organisation and changed it, for the better, almost overnight. It was masterclass in establishing a way of operating that got total buy-in. He made people feel a part of things, that their contribution whether a player, a coach or a member of the general staff was important.

His first words to us all were *"From now on the words, 'please' and 'thank you', travel everywhere with us!"* It seemed innocuous at the time but it altered the atmosphere. We had a talented group; the players individually were very good but we weren't a particularly strong 'team.' Two things he did changed that.

Firstly he brought in two overseas signings from his native Australia, who it is fair to say didn't receive universal approval from the fan base. They were looking for big, star names but Brad Godden and Marc Glanville embodied everything he looked for in an individual. Don't get me wrong they were wonderful players and became firm, fan favourites, but it was their approach that stood out. They were committed and tough with a never say die attitude. They put the team first, they raised the standards on and off the pitch. They wouldn't accept second best and were always looking to improve themselves and those around them. It took the team to another level; Graham had laid out his vision and how we were going to go about achieving it. Just like his insistence on saying please and thank you, where appropriate, he also introduced another simple rule. Whenever we ate meals together, in the canteen, a hotel or a restaurant he insisted that you took the first available chair at the nearest table (players or staff). Instead of sitting down with your mates you now had to sit wherever the first free space was. It broke down many barriers and fostered that togetherness that good teams always have.

Graham built the culture that led to a great deal of success and initially he policed it hard, making sure no one strayed from the accepted standards. In one memorable episode he jumped in his car and chased a player down to the next set of traffic lights after he observed him throwing a banana skin out of his car window onto the grass verge. It wasn't an act he expected of his players and needless to say it wasn't repeated. It was amazing how quickly his standards, behaviours and values became everyone's. The players took things forward, they policed themselves, they drove the standards and this allowed the coach to oversee and focus on other things. I stayed at the club for a year after he left and it was noticeable how standards slipped without his drive. Strong characters build strong cultures and if I've learned anything over the years *"It Starts With Me But Ends With We!"*

DAMIAN MCGRATH

CHANGE
LEAD IT OR MANAGE IT?

Every time a new coach comes in there are the same issues for players and staff.

In sport, usually the changes are traumatic, public sackings, pressure for results, fingers pointed etc. That being the case the environment that a new leader enters is often far from perfect. Players and staff are unsure of their position. It's the same things we all deal with when change occurs. Is their skill set and their style what the new coach wants? Will the new coach's leadership style and management approach be different? Will they be too authoritarian? Are they micro-managers? Will they provide support and guidance? A new leader often brings changes to the work culture, and employees may worry about how these changes will impact their day-to-day work environment, team dynamics, and overall job satisfaction. They wonder if their previous efforts and hard work will be acknowledged and appropriately rewarded.

It is always seemed obvious to me that each new role has to be dealt with carefully. The points above happen in everyday life and it has always seemed common sense that it's not just managing the change from one coach to another or from a new regime to another but leading it. Change is inevitable we all have to deal with it, it happens in all walks of life. As Einstein's famous quote goes about the definition of insanity *"Doing everything the same but expecting things to change"*. Or the variation, *"if you train the way you've always trained you will play the way you've always played."* They basically tell us that to improve or move forward we have to change.

To manage change we deal with the process, how it's going to work, who sits at what desk, the posters, the new timetable, we basically look at the tools to make change happen. Leading change is about the vision, creating a sense of urgency, speaking to the hearts and minds of your staff and players. You have to inspire and motivate people to embrace the change, align the team with a compelling vision, and encourage a culture of adaptability and innovation. Coaches set the direction, communicate the change vision, and empower people to be proactive participants in the journey. I found it much easier to approach change from their perspective not mine. You have to tailor your message not just to those who are on board from the start, but also to those who need a little more persuasion. But one thing's for certain once you grab their attention, don't let go, keep the message front and centre every day.

The most powerful influencers are great at planting dominant thoughts in people's minds and then coming back and watering them as you would a seedling. To be a great influencer you have to be prepared. Show up prepared to have the right conversations, get clarity, if you have a meeting or a conversation you must have an outcome. The best influencers I have met are very outcome focussed, that means people leave them with a positive outlook. You don't get a successful outcome by just doing an activity you get it by design. You can't do it all alone, think strategically about influence, select a leadership group. If you get the right people in the room, they will have a lot of influence out of the room because people will listen to them. Selecting a leadership group could be difficult but take the time to look around at who you have. Who has the most influence? How interested are they in your plan? Do they care enough to want success? Find people who can make decisions and influence people so that you're not in every conversation. You just have to make sure the right conversations are happening about the right things. You create value, build trust and responsibility. Ideally, effective change involves a combination of strong leadership and skilful management. Coaches who effectively lead change, inspire their team and staff, drive innovation and navigate the challenges that come with change to achieve the desired outcomes. Those who solely focus on managing change may struggle with engagement and support.

The best example I ever saw of this was in my early teaching days. A new Headmaster was appointed at a school where I was on a temporary contract covering a lady on maternity leave. The old Headmistress was retiring after twenty-five years at the school. It was a well-regarded school and, as is so often the case, had a core group of staff that had also been there for many years. The talk in the staffroom was one of concern. The new man in charge had spoken with us all as a group and laid out his way of operating, outlining some of the changes he intended to make and who would be doing what. I was an interested spectator as I was only going to be there short term but for the majority of teachers this was a big upheaval. They were used to and happy with how life had been. Suddenly there were changes to the timetable, not huge but different. Assemblies were changed, classrooms were reconfigured and most difficult for many it seemed was a change in the year groups they were assigned to teach. None of this as young teacher at the beginning of my career seemed a big deal but it was such a big deal to the majority. Communication was all about the logistics of the proposed change. Equipment, furniture, posters, meeting times etc. How it was going to happen instead of why it was happening. At no point did I hear 'why' things were being changed and this was the sticking point. What was trying to be achieved? The changes seemed to be without reason, the staff didn't feel their experience and know-how was valued, the new man hadn't canvassed their thoughts or ideas, they were becoming resistors. A simple lack of engagement made them feel they were being ignored and was quickly leading to them being disengaged.

The new Headmaster was a new headmaster! It was his first appointment. He was keen and wanted to make an impact, he knew what he wanted to do and he more than likely knew why, the problem was he didn't communicate it to everyone else. He obviously didn't realise that people will only be willing to follow you on the journey if you are honest, open, and authentic throughout the process. He certainly didn't paint a clear and confidence inspiring vision of the future and the very people he needed to make things happen felt threatened. It was an uncomfortable first few months and the strained relationships were obvious. Improvement only happened as he made the effort to get to know his people and eventually understand their views, their hopes and their fears. Many of the changes he implemented were good and their impact on daily school life were only for the better, in my opinion, but by just implementing and managing the changes instead of leading the way with clarity and enthusiasm he made a positive into a very difficult situation. If you want to drive change and influence change you have to be prepared for the conflict that may come with it.

"A leader takes people where they want to go. A great leader takes people where they don't necessarily want to go but ought to be." – Rosalynn Carter.

CURIOSITY

Have you ever been somewhere or come across something and immediately seen possibilities?

You start to imagine! Imagination fuels our creativity, it translates novel ideas, it makes connections, and sees outcomes that have not yet materialised. I had that feeling when I first met up with The Canadian National Sevens team at a training camp in Florida. I had recently been appointed as Head Coach of a team that had narrowly avoided relegation and failed miserably to qualify for the 2016 Olympic games. Several senior members had retired and the players I met in Sarasota were low on confidence and wary of the new guy!

I was struck by the size of the players. I had some big athletic men in the group. There was plenty of speed and their agility was striking. Their skill set was generally good and although it lacked polish and consistency there was plenty to work with – I was excited by what we could be!

The great thing about training camps is the ability to socialise in a more relaxed manner and I took advantage of this to try and get to know everyone. I discovered young men who cared about playing for their country, who thought deeply about the game, wanted to be successful and were frustrated about their performances both as a team and as individuals. My imagination began to run wild. I had players with the attributes to play an "all court" game, that is a style of play that is a composite of all the different playing styles e.g., open, direct, power, compact etc. I began to formulate game plans in my mind against different teams.

I was curious to find out their views on the best way to play but also to discover whether they had the capabilities to adapt to different approaches.

Curiosity is a natural human characteristic that inclination to explore, investigate, and question things, driven by that question you ask yourself *"I wonder if...?"*

It sends you off in pursuit of discovery with a willingness to explore unfamiliar territories, challenge assumptions, and embrace new ideas. I was curious about the players and staff I was working with, who were they? What was their world view? How open minded were they? I was equally curious about what could possibly be achieved if we changed our approach to suit the array of talent at our disposal.

Curiosity fuels inspiration and creativity. It encourages us to explore new ideas, challenge assumptions, and think outside the box. It ignites our imagination, allows us to see new possibilities. Of course, those new possibilities rely on people and you have to be curious about the people you have before you explore what might be. Curiosity plays a vital role in building meaningful connections with others. It prompts us to genuinely listen, understand different perspectives, and ask the right questions. We learn of their experiences, cultures, and backgrounds so we can develop empathy and respect. By being genuinely interested in other people we can develop stronger relationships, promote understanding, and foster a sense of togetherness. I knew that 'togetherness' was vital if we were to play the style, I felt would bring us success.

Over that first camp I laid out my vision, I explained what I thought we could achieve and what we needed to do to get there. I carefully introduced how I thought we could do it.

Curiosity works both ways they were equally curious as to why I thought this was the best way forward. "Why" is a common question that arises from curiosity. When we ask "why," we are seeking an explanation or understanding of a particular concept. I wanted them to ask rather than just be told. I needed them to search for the underlying reasons, the logic and purpose behind what we would do. A good leader provides context, and as I have said previously it's amazing what people will do if they see a value in doing it.

I always use the Latin phrase "Cui Bono?" it means "To Whom is it a benefit?" It is most often used in a legal setting about identifying crime suspects. It expresses the view that crimes are often committed to benefit their perpetrators. But when you sell your vision, spelling out who benefits from what is to come and how is vitally important, outlining that what we are about to undertake is of benefit to everyone.

What I am always keen to stress is that curiosity is a two-way street. My curious mindset has encouraged a lifelong journey of exploration and discovery, exploring the possibilities and potential rather than dwelling on problems or limitations. But if its only me that's curious in what we can achieve we can't progress too far. I encourage players and staff to ask questions, explore new ideas, and be open to learning from various sources. By doing so, you can create a dynamic and innovative team that thrives on continuous improvement.

It was Voltaire who said *"Judge a man by his questions rather than by his answers"* and both staff and players in the Canadian set up asked great questions that stimulated debate that fostered a 'let's do it' attitude. Together we shared the journey into an exciting future, discovering what we were capable of and enjoying every minute.

Many people fear change, they see it as a threat. The challenge with changes comes from our tendency to see them as problems rather than opportunities for learning and growth. Most people are afraid of changing their routines as they feel comfortable. I read somewhere that people don't fear change as much losing predictability in their lives. Whenever I have started a new role, I have always been mindful of how my new colleagues and the players would see my arrival and my plans. To try and minimise the discomfort I encourage them to be curious in return. In an ideal world everyone would see what you could see, would recognise the possibilities, but that isn't always the case. I have always identified key influencers, most likely the leadership group, to help drive the new direction. I always use them to test new ideas, new approaches and to read the mood of the team. In Samoa they were crucial to developing coach-player interaction, in Germany they helped overcome the 'Doubt Percentage", in Canada they embraced curiosity and shared the excitement of a new beginning.

The success we had together over the coming years was satisfying, our improved world standing and cup successes were built on our collective curiousness about what was possible. How we trained and when we trained, our rest and recovery, injury rehabilitation and prevention and team selection was scrutinised and questioned by a brilliant staff who were equally as curious as me as to what we could do. But the imagination of the players, who could take the ideas and explore them was so often the difference between winning and losing.

A curious me imagined once upon a time what might lie beyond the horizon. But I didn't leave it there. It is a mindset that propels us forward, opens doors to new possibilities, and enriches our overall life experience. It has to be part of our everyday life or we aren't really living!

DON'T LET SIMPLICITY FOOL YOU

"What we see depends mainly on what we look for".
John Lubbock

In the midst of the Australian Rugby League team's tour of England in 1994 I was asked to organise an open training session. I have mentioned previously how much interest those tours created. To the British RL fan, it was a rare opportunity to see the famous names in the flesh as we could only read of the game's big stars from down-under. TV coverage was rare, so when they were in town everyone, it seemed, wanted to see them in action.

I had had the great good fortune to be appointed as the Team's Liaison Officer which as an aspiring coach was 'manna from heaven' as I got to see them up-close and personal on a daily basis. I was inundated with requests from the general public to attend training sessions, so I asked the team manager if we could hold an open session to satisfy the many people who wanted to attend.

I was given the green light to organise open access at the training session the following Monday morning. It was being held at the home of one of Rugby Leagues most famous clubs, Castleford RLFC.

It was an ideal venue situated in the heartland of the game and easily accessible across the north of England. Several thousand people attended, many of them coaches as well as fans, all wanting to see the worlds greatest players train and learn the secrets of their success. I was stood at the back of the main stand as the team came out to warm-up. As they began their first drill you could literally hear pages in hundreds of notebooks being opened as pens prepared to write the key points.

The two men next to me were poised, I smiled at their focus. The team began using a simple drill, the ball was being passed around the square. It began slowly and got quicker, the players on command went out to make the square bigger or came in to make it smaller. passes were high, low or normal, or even changed direction. It was a thing of beauty! Not once was the ball dropped, not once did the quality drop, not once did the communication or focus waver. It reminded me of synchronised swimming, a whole team working in complete harmony at bewildering speed it seemed. They finished the warm-up and grabbed drinks before the main part of the session was to begin.

The bloke next to me turned to his friend looking slightly perplexed. *"What did you think of that?"* he said. *"Rubbish"*, said his mate *"We do that drill at our training!"* He was underwhelmed to say the least!

Like many, they had completely missed the lesson. Yes, I'm sure it was the same practice they did with their team, but it was how they did it! That was the key! For some reason they expected the world's best Rugby League players in the world's best Rugby League team to do something completely different to everyone else. It wasn't what they did it was how they did it which they should have noted. There is no magic bullet, they just executed the fundamentals on a different level. As Booker T. Washington says *"Excellence is the ability to do the common thing in an uncommon way"*.

I have come across many coaches who manage training. That is, they set up their cones and balls etc. explain what is expected to happen and then stand back and let it run. They keep everyone moving and shout general words of encouragement or criticism as they see fit. The smart coaches, coach everything. The practice, no matter how simple, isn't relevant unless it has learning moments, they look past the mechanics of a drill or game and focus on the key points that are the reason it's being done. One of the differences between the best coaches and the less experienced is how they look past the obvious to derive the most from any practice, because as David Thoreau says *"It's not what you look at it is what you see."*

BE HAPPY WITH WHO YOU ARE?

What do you see when you look in a mirror?

I always get a shock, particularly when I glance in one rather than deliberately look. Who is that person – it's not me surely? In my mind's eye I'm still 25. I still laugh at the same things, I still love clothes, music, TV programmes etc. Me and my pals still giggle at the same stupid things, we still appreciate an attractive lady, we still love a night out and still talk a better game of football than we ever played! Unfortunately, I still have the same appetite but not the body to carry the calorific intake.

So, it still shocks me that I look like a bloke in his 60's. But only for a second because it doesn't really matter. I also noticed recently that I smile at myself in the mirror. I am not sure why, am I sharing a joke only me, myself and I get? Or am I just happy at where life has taken me and the person I have become. When you are younger you worry far more how you look and on the judgements of other people but as you age (gracefully or not) you tend to be more concerned with your own view of yourself.

I have finally come to the conclusion that time and experience should give you satisfaction with yourself. It has taken me a long time to be happy with who I am. My journey, my adventures have allowed me to become more secure in myself and my abilities. I've gained a broader perspective on life. I realise the opinions of others are subjective and can be influenced by various factors. This wisdom helps me take other people's judgments with a pinch of salt and I don't let them dictate my self-worth. I spend less time seeking approval from others. I've learned to focus on what truly matters to me and I'm less concerned about meeting others' expectations. I've become more accepting of my imperfections and those of others. I've realised that nobody is perfect, including me, it's given me a more forgiving and non-judgmental attitude towards myself and others. I thought that my mission was solely to help others become a better version of themselves but that was just a byproduct of me finding a contented version of myself. As my hero, the late, great, David Bowie once said *"Ageing is an extraordinary process where you become the person you always should have been"*

CONCLUSION

I came across an article on twitter by Billy Oppenheimer. It was about the multi-award-winning movie director James Cameron.

In 1991 when James Cameron's movie, *Terminator 2,* was riding high as the top grossing movie of that year, he was asked by an aspiring young film maker *"How do you become a successful film director?"* Cameron himself had received no formal training so he was a good man to ask. Cameron replied, *"If you have to ask, you'll probably never do it"* He gave two reasons.

Firstly, he quoted Syd Field, who in his book on screenwriting, wrote that the core trait of all great characters is that character's "dramatic need." With a "dramatic need" – to get something, to go somewhere, or to beat somebody – the character persists through the story's obstacles, problems and conflicts. To be a successful film director, Cameron says, you need to have a dramatic need. Like a good story the filmmaking process is a relentless series of obstacles, problems and conflicts. If you're discouraged by this then you clearly don't have the dramatic need to persist.

Secondly, he said that of all the successful filmmakers he knew, no two people did it the same way. Their career trajectories were shaped by their own unique strengths and weaknesses. *"Whatever your strengths and weaknesses"* Cameron said *"you have to find the path that's going to work for you."* The idea is to seek your own path not someone else's!

All the best coaches have a dramatic need. They strive to overcome the challenges they meet, to get something and go somewhere. They seek the information and knowledge to forge their own path. They innovate, they're curious, they're resilient, authentic and much, much more, they really are a 'man for all seasons.' If I had to try and think of a key attribute it would be persistence. There is very rarely a linear progression in anyone's life. The path I forged was anything but straight. The obstacles, problems and conflicts have always been there. I had to find a way through and it sometimes it necessitated stepping to one side or even going backwards, but importantly I never stopped moving. Was I 'Fluent In Success?' I don't know but what has become apparent to me as time has gone by is that I have always tried to leave places better than I found them and if I could be viewed in that way, I would leave the coaching stage a very satisfied man.

In my loft at home I have, like I'm sure a lot of people have, boxes full of memorabilia. Things I have collected on my journey. Playing shirts, press clippings, photographs, cups, medals etc. A physical reminder of great times past. But my two most treasured items are an email and a twitter message.

I had a notification on my twitter account in August 2022. It said I had a message request and would I accept it. I did and found the message below. I have edited out the name but it was from a boy (well, a middle-aged man now) I had taught at the beginning of my coaching journey at Shakespeare Middle School 40 years ago.

Hi Sir yes Sir always be that to me Mr McGrath you had a massive impact on all our lives when we played under you at rugby under 11s at Shakespeare you made us feel like we could take on the world some days,just an amazing human being always very fair and also hard on us when we deserved it. Even to this day you was the greatest teacher by a country mile and everyone who you taught still speaks very highly sir.Just want to take this opportunity to say thank you Mr McGrath and I we treasure the memories we had playing Rugby league under you.Hope you remember me ▓▓ ▓▓▓▓ 💜 💜 💜 💜 Take. Care and God bless xxx

It stopped me in my tracks it was better than any award. Could I possibly have asked for anymore?

Amidst a political upheaval at Rugby Canada in 2019 I was one of a number of staff sacked. It was a tough time, as my wife and I had established a good life there, we were settled and the team had been successful. It's never nice to lose your job and even if you feel it's unwarranted, the soul searching that follows, can cause you to question your competence and look at your own shortcomings. We were both overwhelmed with support both publicly and privately. It was very welcome and rewarding to know that despite what had happened we were well thought of. But just before I boarded the plane back to England, I received an email; It was from the whole Canadian team, a letter of recommendation!

Canadian National 7s Team
3024 Glen Lake Rd Victoria,
BC V9B 4B4

May 15, 2019

To Whom It May Concern,

I write this letter of recommendation on behalf of the entire Men's Canadian National 7's Team in regards to Damian McGrath. Damian worked with all of us for the past two and a half years as the head coach of the Canadian National 7's Team.

Damian was introduced to our team at a time when the culture and on-field performances were at an all time low. Many senior players decided to move on from the team after a tough few years with the previous coach. Along with the lack of player depth, there had also been funding cuts, so the situation Damian was presented with was less than ideal.

Damian had an immediate impact on the team as he subtly created a very positive team culture and training environment. He truly bought in to the Canadian culture and was quickly accepted by not only the team but the entire Canadian rugby community. His commitment to helping grow not only the 7s program, but also rugby across Canada, is something that has not been seen from an international coach in our Canadian rugby community. He devoted an unbelievable amount of time, outside of long tours and training blocks, to travel back and forth across Canada helping grow the game we love. To have that kind of impact in such a short period of time is a testament to the kind of person Damian is, someone who puts the interests of the players and the rugby community first.

Damian was instrumental in our success on the world stage by empowering and motivating each and every athlete, day in and day out, to reach levels we had not seen before. The numerous top performances against the best teams in the world, in a very short period of time, shows the immediate impact he made, producing a record year for the Canadian 7's program. Canadian rugby history was made under the direction of Damian, winning the first ever World Series Title in Singapore!

Damian's unwavering dedication to the players and staff was an invaluable part of our rugby family and his loss has had an immediate impact which we all, players, staff and rugby community, felt and continue to feel. Personally, after playing rugby at the National level for over 10 years, I have seen few people with the desire to help athletes and grow the game similar to Damian. He went above and beyond to provide for everyone around him. To say that Damian was a valuable part of our team and Canadian rugby would be a massive understatement, and the value that he brings to any environment is priceless.

If you are reading this then you are most likely considering hiring Damian for a position within your organisation. Please do not make the mistake of passing up on someone who will not only make a positive impact, but will help build your team or organisation with his genuine characteristics, expertise in his discipline, and love for what he does.

Sincerely,
The entire Men's Canadian National 7's Team

I hope you don't mind me sharing them with you. One is from the start and one towards the end of my coaching career. To me personally they mean the world and I include them not as a, *"Look how great I am"*, type of thing but a reminder that really, as Maya Angelou said, *"People will forget what you said, people will forget what you did, but people will never forget how you made them feel."*

DAMIAN MCGRATH

BIOGRAPHY

Damian McGrath played professional Rugby League for Batley. He has coached professionally at domestic, national and international level across both codes of rugby. His first coaching opportunity came at Batley where he led the Reserve team to overdue success. This led to an invitation to join Leeds RL as Academy Coach. After several successful seasons he was appointed to be Assistant 1st Team Coach at Leeds, followed by a similar role at London Broncos. During this period he gained international recognition, firstly coaching the Great Britain Academy RL team then as Assistant Coach for the Great Britain U21s, before becoming the Assistant Coach for the Senior National Team at the 2000 Rugby League World Cup.

He became one of the first coaches to change codes when he joined the England Rugby Union set up at the turn of the millennium. He was appointed Skills and Defence Coach for the England Sevens and England 'A' teams. Alongside this he held a similar role with Leicester Tigers 1st team. He was Assistant Coach for the England U19s who won bronze at the World Cup and was Head Coach of the Junior England Sevens team that won a silver medal at the Junior Commonwealth Games in Australia. During this period England Sevens appeared at the Sevens World Cup and the Commonwealth Games in Manchester as well as winning the prestigious Hong Kong Sevens on four consecutive occasions.

He was Skills and defence coach for the Spanish National Rugby team for three years before becoming Head of Rugby for the North Wales Rugby Region (RGC).

He returned to become Assistant Coach of England Sevens, including another appearance at the Commonwealth Games in Glasgow. In

2014 he was Head coach of Great Britain Students team that won a gold medal at the World Student Games in Brazil.

In 2015 he became Head Coach of the Samoan National Sevens team leading them to a Cup success in Paris. He then took over as Head Coach of the Canadian National Sevens team leading them to a historic Cup success in Singapore. He also coached the team in the Commonwealth Games in Brisbane and the Sevens World Cup in San Francisco.

On returning to Europe, he took over as Head Coach of the German National Sevens team leading them to victory in the World Challenger Series in Chile followed by an unprecedented fifth place finish in a World Series event. He then took over as Kenya National Sevens team coach leading them to the Sevens World Cup in Cape Town and the Commonwealth games in Birmingham.

He attained a B.Ed degree whilst training to be a teacher and spent two years on Personal Development at Ashridge Business School.

He has been a key note speaker at several national and international events including the 2012 Olympics and written three, well-received, rugby skills books.

The beginning with celebrations
at Batley.

Shakespeare Middle School. Where
my fledgling coaching career began.

Celebrating a Wembley victory with
Graham Murray.

Its not just winning its enjoying.

Embracing other cultures is always
important.

The immeasurable joy of success.
Samoans made every minute
unforgettable.

I am not so sure I am happy!

The winning moment! The elation captured as the hooter signals Samoa's incredible victory over Fiji in Paris.

Communication is more than just words.

Prince Albert of Monaco was a big fan
of Manu Samoa.

There are times when precise
information is required.

Pre-game information with Kenya.

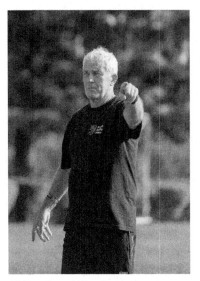

Although coaching is a two way street, leaders must give direction.

Samoan boys saying farewell to my wife and I.

Post-game feedback in Las Vegas.

Pre-game pictures and words, when less is more.

A smile can make a big difference.

A historic moment in Canadian rugby history.

Canadian players threw a farewell BBQ for my wife and I. So sad to leave these wonderful people but so glad to have had the chance to be part of their lives.

Printed in Great Britain
by Amazon

34318230R00099